AGES
OF
ELEGANCE

SBN 356/02504/7

AGES
OF
ELEGANCE

FIVE THOUSAND YEARS
OF FASHION
AND FRIVOLITY

GISÈLE D'ASSAILLY

MACDONALD-LONDON

This book should be dedicated to elegant women throughout the world, for it will take them on a fascinating journey through fashion over the centuries.

Gisèle d'Assailly tells us how and why fashion changes according to the whim of a king or a courtezan, the discovery of a continent or a silkworm cocoon. She describes day to day life at the Courts of Knossos or of King Solomon, the pageantry of Francis I or of Elizabeth the First of England. She reveals the beauty secrets of Egyptian women, the shapes of Greek wigs, of Cypriot sandals or the Roman brassiere... Thanks to her, we discover that Cretan women were the first to display wasp-waists, to wear hooped bell-dresses and little boots like those of our grandmothers. We learn that Henry II was the first French King to wear earrings and that the Jardin des Plantes was created in Henry IV's reign in order to give new inspiration to the silk-weavers. In a word, we are lead on a fascinating survey of male and female fashions, their elegance, luxury and diversity. And we can dream of yesterday's follies while musing upon those of tomorrow.

Nicole Hervé Alphand.

5

Speaking of women, a wit described them as "charming little things for whom men risk their honor, ruin and even kill themselves and whose sole concern in the midst of this universal slaughter is with dressing up either like umbrellas or like bells."

7

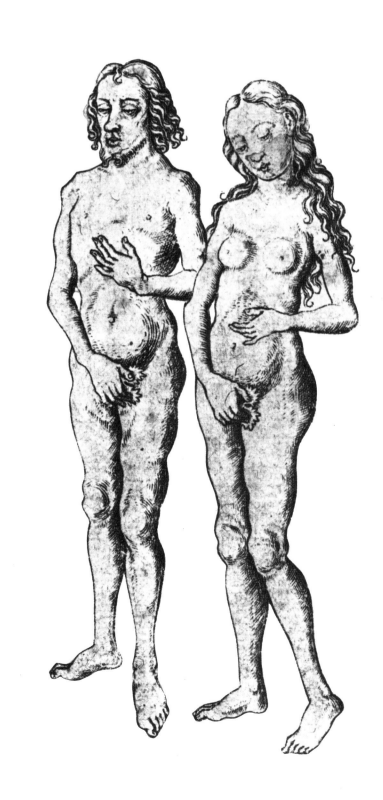

To Sophie and Diane

*The history of elegance is rather like a fairy tale peopled by magiciens,
covered with precious stones, flimsily-clad shepherdesses,
queens majestically draped in court dresses and princesses barely veiled in transparent muslin.
Fashion is both unexpected and constant, gay and melancholy,
frivolous and wise.   Let me take your hand and lead you,
like Alice in Wonderland, into this strange and marvellous world.*

BY GISÈLE D'ASSAILLY.

THE KAUNAKES

THE FIRST REVOLUTION

THE KAUNAKE OF MESOPOTAMIA

Garments such as the sable cape and the fashionable bear coat were as coveted 160,000 years ago as they are today. Perhaps even more so, for furs were the only clothing known to man or woman those many millennia ago. Indeed, they were the first clothing, and made their appearance on the backs of the hardy hunters of reindeer and mammouths. Needless to say these garments lacked the svelt opulence of today's intricately draped pelts, for the curing of the skins was accomplished simply by drying them in the sun. Then, too, the fur was not considered to be a costly and somewhat useless luxury. It was just a skin that was found to be a convenient protection for another and more fragile skin.

This rough and ready fashion varied little during the whole paleolithic period. The fight for survival left little time or energy for frivolities. But, as

Neolithic cave paintings from Saltadora, Spain, depict (from left to right):
The Hunt.
The Herd.
The War Dance.

the human mind expanded, tools were invented and with technological progress — tools such as fish hooks and shaped stones used for cutting — elegance made a timid appearance. The tangled hair of the animal skins was combed, and the hide cut into strips. This first fashion is called the kaunake. It was to be a long-lived style that would find its way into most of the civilized areas of the ancient world until it eventually evolved out of existence around 2000 B.C. in Mesopotamia, an area which was a veritable beehive of fashionable innovations on the theme of the kaunake. This region, a blessed land miraculously protected from wind and cold, made up of plains and valleys irrigated by the Tigris and Euphrates Rivers, provided the kind of conditions needed for the evolution of civilization, hence of elegance.

The Semites, probably the first on the scene, arrived about 4000 B.C. in the Upper and Middle Euphrates valleys. The Akkadians, a farming people, conquered them. Five centuries later, a trading people, the Sumerians settled, and created a civilization which even today captures our admiration when we contemplate the artistry of the objects found

at the sites of the ancient kingdoms of Uruk, Susa, Lagash and Mari.

For people less favored by nature, especially the inhabitants of the high plateaux of the Caucasus, Armenia and Afghanistan, the nomads of Asia Minor or the steppes of northern Europe, Mesopotamia was an enviable land of milk and honey. In fact, the authors of the Old Testament saw it as the location of Paradise on earth. Periodically, the peoples less well-situated burst like waves upon this paradise. The result: a mixture of races, a certain disorder but also a considerable enrichment. Then too, during the fourth millennium, the kingdoms of Mari and Lagash were active traders, their ships and caravans plying the countries of the Indus and the coastal areas around the Caspian Sea and the Eastern Mediterranean. This also served to introduce new cloths and styles of clothing into Mesopotamia. The little kingdoms lived together in harmony as no single ruler became strong enough to dominate the others. Consequently, the residents could exchange ideas and invent others so that in the realm of fashion, the kaunake underwent a series of modifications, sometimes a century apart,

during the second half of the third millennium, before this basic garment finally disappeared.

Indeed, the kaunake played such a basic role in the life of ancient man, that its importance surpasses that of a simple garment.

The term served originally to designate a sheep or goat skin which had been made into a garment in the region of Asia Minor. Then thanks to the invention of the cutting stone, this simple covering became decorative. It was shaved in spots, combed like a royal poodle, cut in small strips and even fringed. At the end of the mesolithic period, man invented weaving. Wool was woven into a course material and fashioned into the same line as the primitive kaunake. This fabric, tightly or loosely woven and arranged in vertical strips or horizontal flounces resembles the goat-hair blankets found today in the Atlas Mountains. It was also used by two very different prehistoric civilizations separated by two thousand years. Between 3200 B.C. and 1200 B.C. the Celts in Europe and the nomads of ancient Asia both wore the roughly woven kaunake. The Celts made a waterproof raincoat out of it, the rain running off the long hairs.

The Sumerians, including the kings of Mari fashioned the kaunake into a loin-cloth skirt which they fastened at their waist much like an apron. A belt terminated in a knob or tassel, a survival of the even more ancient notion that the skin of an animal tied around the waist by its tail bestowed power upon its wearer. The citizens of Tell el-Armana on the Nile River wore a kaunake that ended mid-calf in a deep flounce. Servants wore mini-kaunakes ending at the knee.

The kaunake disappeared from the fashion scene about 2000 B.C. But traces of it are to be found in the Middle Ages, and even today, the same fabric can be seen in Asia Minor.

Our "yeyes" of today, who think themselves to be the epitome of modernism are in fact but pale imitator of the Assyrians who, 3000 years ago, wore their hair down to their shoulders. They preferred long- sideburns or beards squared off and falling on the chest in several rows of curls arranged like truffles on the Christmas turkey. The rest of the face was carefully shaven. At the court of Mari, protocol prescribed the coiffure. Certain dignitaries wore their hair straight down their backs with the end twisted into a curl. As abundance of hair was a symbol of strength, those — especially kings — who were not so blessed by nature are thought to have worn wigs and false beards in the manner of pharaohs. As for the waves and curls so typical of this court, they were probably created with a curling iron.

The women of Mari were more independent and apparently liked to frequently change their hair styles. Sometimes they wore their hair flowing down the back and sometimes it was caught in a hairnet or a pleated scarf and worn in a chignon. The coquettes of the day had a thousand tricks to make themselves more seductive: some wove ribbons through their chignons, others cut short their hair, waving it close to the head while others curled a few

(left to right):

Ebil II, steward to the King of Mari in the third millenium B.C. wears a kaunake. (Louvre Museum.)

A bronze from the Sumerian city of Lagash portrays Prince Goudea in a robe from 2350 B.C.

Queen Napir of Susa wears a gown circa 1500 B.C.

locks tightly over the ears, allowing the rest of the hair to fall to their shoulders. Gold pins were stuck in here and there, and the ladies also wore necklaces and rings.

The men, however, were more austere in their dress. They wore no jewelry and walked barefooted. Nevertheless, a shoe with a slightly pointed toe was found in a tomb dating from 3000 B.C. Much like a Turkish shoe, it also appears on several seals from Akkad. Kings apparently wore them but only when dressed in their robes of state. Possibly invading mountain tribes introduced them into the region and they were adopted first in order to provide a firmer foothold and later as a decorative adornment.

The art of the third millennium generally took inspiration from religious ceremonies but these representations also give us information on the fashions of the day. Thus among the worshippers in the ancient Sumerian city of Khafaje, we see kings wearing kaunake skirts, their torsos bare and their shoulders firmly square. The women, often represented in a sitting position are dressed in asymetrical robes leaving the right shoulder uncovered. Others wear a sort of cape with ruffles that covers the entire body. One of the most astounding garments found in Mesopotamia is that of the "great singer, Ur Mina", a citizen of Mari in the first half of the third millenium. We see her sitting in her robe which ends in pantaloons caught above the knee — the first bloomers ! Were they made of kaunake type cloth or of fine linen ? Was the lady a singer or a dancer ? I think that Ur Mina must have swung the hip if not the guitar. A statuette representing the goddess of Ur wears a charming neckline bordered with a sort of raised piping which leaves her shoulders free and plunges between her breasts. As to the queen reigning over Ur in 4000 B..C, her coiffure decorated with gold flowers would please our hippies of today. A goddess of Mari wore a capelet composed of six necklaces made of semi-precious stones. On her ears, large earrings. The queens and goddesses of the day were indeed conscious of their charms. Our divinity of Mari was dressed in a short-sleeved dress, the skirt raised just enough to show her dainty bare feet. As to her strange hairdo, it is made of crisscross locks puffed out so that one is reminded of a colonial helmet. There was relatively little difference in the styles worn by the two sexes for a period of more than five hundred years. Small details were all that marked the sex of the wearer. The elegant ladies of Susa, for instance, wore luxurious shawls with intricate trimmings. But during the period of Sargon, the Semitic officer who overthrew the Sumerian Empire about 2,300, women became more feminine, draping shawls with greater grace over their short-sleeved robes. Peasants wore the same costume, but held it in at the waist with a padded belt. During the third and second millenniums, men wore a short tunic which they pulled on over their heads. The sleeves were long and narrow. The ever-present shawl was draped in the same manner as the Greeks were later to use, but only kings were permitted to wear it under one arm and thrown across the other shoulder. The shawls of officials were pleated and edged with a fringe whose length varied according to the importance of the wearer, much as directors of companies demonstrate their position by driving a Cadillac or a Rolls Royce.

In order to have an idea of the standard of elegance of about 1500 B.C., we must describe the robe of the queen of Susa, Napir Asou. She wears a bell-shaped skirt mounted on a corselet. The sleeves are long and narrow, held at the wrist by embroidery. A shawl is thrown casually over a shoulder and draped around her hips. The bottom of her skirt is edged with a fringe that touches her feet.

Although the Sumerian, Babylonian and Assyrian clothes were lavishly embroidered and fringed, the colors were dull ochres, browns and pale yellows, until Phoenician traders introduced the brilliant reds and the famous purples made from a shellfish a called whelk. The materials were mostly wool and linen. They are covered with squared designs or circles of embroidery. In the center of each, a gold, agate or cornaline bead.

Judging from the painted pottery and the wall murals, the colors most frequently used in the second and third millenniums seemed to have been green, red and yellow as well as somber blue and burnt sienna. But it is difficult to get a clear idea of the materials for the Mesopotamian climate was more humid than that of Egypt, and the cloth rotted away. Then too, the Sumerians buried their dead naked in order that the clothing would not offend the gods. The demands and needs attributed to the many deities must indeed have regulated the standards of elegance.

THE SECOND REVOLUTION
THE PAINTED EGYPTIANS

According to the French Egyptologist, Gaston Maspero, the delta and valley of the Nile were, during the mesolithic age (10000-5000 B.C.) "occupied by naked hunters and shepherds; their chiefs alone wore panther skins thrown across their shoulders or wrapped around their waists, covering the stomach." The animal skins swept the ground at their heels. Maspero believes that these peoples smeared their limbs with grease and oil, and tattooed at least a part of their faces and bodies.

Ancient paintings and stone carvings show us that, from about the fifth millennium onwards, it was fashionable for both sexes to use black antimony powder to emphasize the arc of their eyebrows. The contours of their eyelids were also lined to extend them as far as their temples. A layer of green paint covered their lower eyelids while cheeks were daubed with ochre and lips with carmine. This fashion was to last for several thousand years.

This green make-up, made from malachite, lasted from the neolithic age, in 5000 B.C. to the 18th Dynasty in 1300 B.C. The paste was both decorative and medicinal for it contained hydrosilicate of copper, a sovereign remedy against the opthalmia and

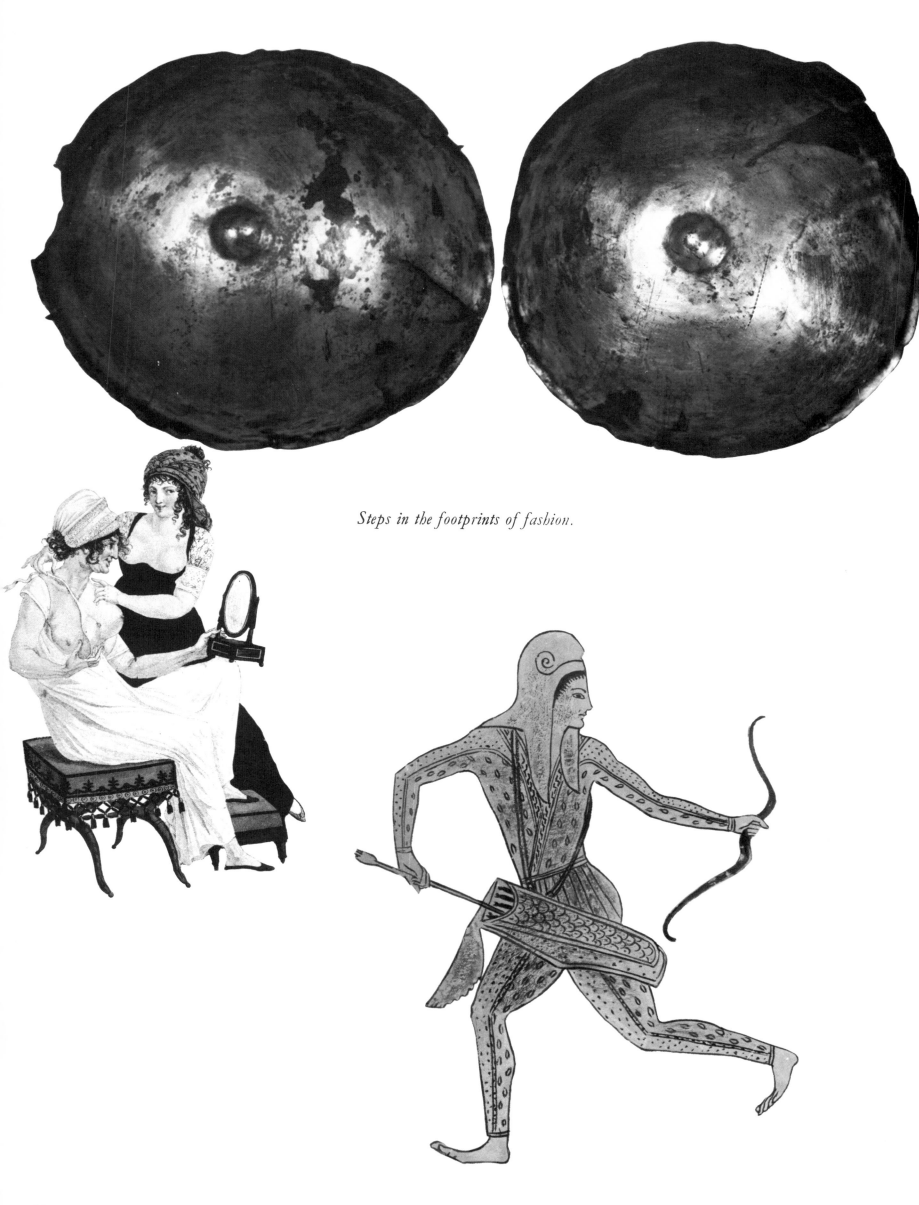

Steps in the footprints of fashion.

suppuration incurred by the north African sun. Children who seemed heavily made up from birth were, in fact, only well cared for. The black make-up drawn from galena which gave such emphatic expression to the eyes is used still today under the name of kohl.

Strange mixtures went into their cosmetics. Egyptian beauties painted the contours of their eyes with a concoction of burnt ants' eggs ground in a mortar. On the other hand, many ointments served not only to hide imperfections but to perfume the skin as well. Tombs dating from 4000 B.C. have revealed alabaster and shale palettes serving for mixing the pastes and ointments before application with a thin spatula, a luxury compared to modern-day methods.

It would be wrong to think that these sophisticated ladies allowed the thick layers to dry on their skin like a crust. On the contrary, they washed far more frequently than most of our contemporaries, when they arose from bed, and before and after meals as well, using a water perfumed with natural hydrocarbonate of soda. In order to clean their pores properly, they rubbed themselves with sand and bathed in deep pools.

A tanned complexion was fashionable, but for certain ceremonies, women covered their faces with a mixture of ceruse and white of egg. This early mask had the advantage of tightening the skin and removing the wrinkles — on the condition that one kept a true poker face.

During the reigns of the Ramses and the Ptolemies, make-up became so violent that it resembled illuminated manuscript coloring. Bright greens mingled with loud purples and provocative ultramarines. Such recipes were contained in the *Cosmetikon*, the golden book of beauty, and their fame spread as far as Rome where the nobility feverishly applied concoctions to the skin in order to have the "dazzle of gold and ivory", and eyes "the depth of the sea".

From the earliest times in Egypt, men and women, almost naked and painted like posters, cut their hair in even tiers. The hair was divided into slender locks which were plaited from the roots to the end. The final effect was of a complicated structure made up of plaits, curls, matted and greased which covered the forehead, temples and the shoulders.

Later on, the Egyptians, no doubt wearied by the problems of assembling this monument of capillary art, decided to wear wigs. Made of silk or horse-hair as natural hair. This was glued, with a kind of tar, onto a canvas which was cut and sewn to the shape of the head, then tinted black or blue and decorated with gold threads or sprigs. These wigs came in every shape and price, and were *de rigueur* for the nobility. Curiously enough, these coquettes, not wishing to be thought bald, allowed some of their natural hair to be seen. Braided or rolled, tiered or puffed out, real or false, the hair often fell to their shoulders. But we also see young girls who served as gift-bearers in the 11th Dynasty, coiffed like Joan of Arc. Elegant women decorated their hairdos, real or false, with crowns or golden diadems studded with tiny flowers,

Fashion repeats itself across the centuries (left to right):

Breast-covers, beginning of the third millennium, were found in a tomb in the city of Susa. (Louvre Museum.)

A lady dons a similar garment. (Bibliothèque Nationale, Paris.)

An archer from the end of the 4th century B.C. already wears a Phrygian bonnet. (British Museum.)

The "Sans culotte" who preferred pantaloons to breeches, in the French Revolution, might have taken his cue from the archer. (Carnavalet Museum.)

lilies or tiny flower-buds. The more refined ladies added a tiny ball of scented ointment which slowly melted during the course of the evening.

With wigs or without them, the Egyptians attached great importance to the beauty of their hair. Recipes have been found to cure baldness as well as to make the rival's hair fall out...

Prince Rasseper of the 5th Dynasty changed his costume at the same time as he changed his wig while the Princess Kaouit in the 11th Dynasty spent hours having her hair curled.

While their owners slept at night, the wigs were placed on stands and guarded by slave girls.

The Egyptians, aside from the love of extravagant make-up and hairdos, also used an incredible quantity of perfume. Aromas were manufactured by priests who burned resins and scented woods to embalm and thus to preserve the corpses in the necropolis.

In due course, these aromatic compounds were perfected and then integrated in religious ceremonies, a practice later picked up by Moses.

Well before the reign of Cheops, builder of the Great Pyramid in 2800 B.C., all the more important temples contained special rooms where perfumes and antiseptics were prepared for use in embalming. The different formulas in use were written on the walls as blackboards did not yet exist.

Later still, priests thought up ways of making a

profit from these scents, and put them on sale despite the law-makers who tried to forbid their use outside the temple. Needless to say, the beauties of the day outbid each other in their desire to buy these most secret mixtures whose formulas had been guarded for centuries. Soon, perfumes became the indispensable complement of the Egyptian woman's dress, a major change in their habits.

This was an era of grace in objects as well. According to the bas-reliefs found in a perfume distillery of Alexandria, the liquids were contained in long-necked retorts resembling ibises.

Between 3000 and 2000 B.C., the neolithic age, the Hittites and Aegians, mostly farmers and herdsmen, settled on the banks of the Nile River in Upper Egypt. They were to remain there for 4000 years. At that time, men and women dressed alike; the entire lower part of the body was moulded by a piece of cloth called the *shentit*. It was designed to enhance the slimness of the hips and the smallness of the waist. Shoulders were bare in order to show them off to their best advantage.

Linen was used not only because it was cool and light-weight but also because of its natural whiteness which bestowed on it a sacred character; on the other hand, wool was considered to be impure by the priests who forbade its use as a burial wrapping. The continuity of style in Egyptian clothing between about 3200 and 1500 B.C. is a constant source

of surprise when one considers the remarkable refinement of these people.

But such continuity was not unique to Egypt. Each nation, whether in Mesopotamia, or in Crete, in Persia or later on in Greece, tended to adopt its own style and to remain faithful to it for centuries. Only the accessories, shoes and coiffures changed, although why this should be so is difficult to understand. One style unique to Egypt was found in the tombs of the Old Empire, of about the middle of the third millenium. It consisted of a wide skirt with horizontal pleats sewn onto a short bodice which had long fitted sleeves. Some had tiny frills under the arms. The more popular fashion was held up by wide shoulder straps, and was gathered in under the breasts in a way that displayed the bosom to good advantage. In addition, a shawl was worn which fastened at the throat. However it is difficult to have an accurate idea of the typical style of dress worn during the Old and New Empires because fashions depicted on later monuments may well have been copied from earlier ones. Nevertheless the continuity is quite apparent. Invasions seemed to have played a relatively minor role in introducing any changes. Likewise, exceptional political and commercial climates had little effect on them. In general, prosperity tends to encourage every sort of excess. Yet, in Egypt, it was in a moment of decline of the power of the Pharaohs, after the departure of the

The stylistic elegance of ancient Egypt is seen here. (Left to right) :

Finely plaited woollen wigs were worn in the New Empire. (British Museum.)

Printed dresses were not invented yesterday. These women, whose dresses we would gladly copy, are Bedouin captives. (Fresco from Beni-Hassan rock tombs - Egypt: 3rd Dynasty.)

Hyskos who had invaded Egypt from Syria in 1680 B.C., that styles began to change. Perhaps the Egyptians, while fighting against this race who considered it immodest to go about bare-breasted, lit on the idea of covering their loin-cloths with a sleeved tunic-dress. Cut out of white transparent linen, it was embellished with a panel of sun burst pleats and was called a "calarisis".

These famous form-fitting pleats were undoubtedly created by means of gum-starching, a process also used by the inhabitants of Asia Minor to stiffen their tunics. The cloth itself was fabricated on vertical frames by highly perfected weaving techniques which permitted fluting, crimping, or undulated forms according to the whims of the customers. Judging by the pieces of fabric found on mummies, these weaving frames were small.

Under the New Empire, from 1580 to 1040 B.C., ladies of high birth continued to wear the old-fashioned sheath held in place by two gold or brightly colored shoulder straps which also served to conceal the breasts. Some women tied these shoulder straps into a bow just above the collarbone like a small butterfly.

These sheaths were woven or embroidered with brightly colored designs of wings and feathers. It is worth noting that colors were very numerous and most delicately shaded in those days.

There were also sari-draped dresses made of a single piece of muslin gathered at the waist and wrapped around the breast. This fashion seems to have been inspired by Phoenician styles which were undoubtedly the predecessors of the Hindu models we see today. There is nothing surprising about this.

It can also be explained by the fact that the Egyptian Empire extended as far as Syria and the Upper Euphrates. Certain statues and paintings show us this kind of dress decorated with many-colored ribbons placed beneath the breasts in order that they be displayed to advantage, and then knotted over the ribs.

Even the working class women of that day were fashion-conscious. Their dresses, which resembled shirts made of white or unbleached cloth, were covered with netting composed of colored beads and caught at the waist by a cord.

Slaves and court dancers were generally naked or at best dressed in a *pagne* or short tunic, in order to preserve their freedom of movement.

In hot climates and at the seaside, the fashionable ladies protected themselves from the sun or the evening breezes by throwing over their shoulders a light-weight woolen shawl. Either white or pale yellow, they were tied or crossed over the breast.

From the 18th Dynasty onwards, Pharaohs stopped wearing a lion's tail attached to their belts as a symbol of power. In its place, they wore the royal Haik. Placed over the skirted *pagne*, this light garment wrapped around the hips, covered the shoulders and tied at the throat. The fabric was either without any design or embroidered with beads of precious or semi-precious stones, or decorated with small gold plaques. Over it, the pharaohs wore piles of gold jewelry, beautifully chased enamels and many-colored belts made of ribbons.

Much of Egyptian jewelry was endowed with special significance. Pharaohs, on feast days wore high tiaras or the truncated hat known as the *Pschant*, as symbols of power. A false beard completed the costume. In fact it was so essential in the portrayal of power that queen Matshrtpdout, who reigned for 21 years, wore one on feast days and even had herself portrayed with the body and clothing of a man but with the features of a woman. Colors in jewelry also had an esoteric significance and must be limited to lapis-lazuli, turquoise blue, cornelian red or faded yellow. Colored beads were combined with pearls and mounted with consummate art and delicacy.

The jewelry worn by the common people was made of glass paste and that of the nobility, of semi-precious stones.

During the 18th Dynasty, a special necklace or throat piece was invented. Made up of two to four rows of gold disks, it was worn against the skin or over the dress. Sometimes, it was embellished with pendants or finished off with a saw-toothed border. During banquets, ornaments of this kind, made of cloth with colored tassels rather than gold, were hung around the necks of the guests by pretty serving girls. Certain documents mention that guests wore "flowers around the neck" and it may be supposed that these necklaces were sometimes made of fresh lotus flowers stuck into the cloth. They can also be seen on frescoes where they seem to float on the skin as though suspended in a miraculous way. Such ornaments could well be offered by a contemporary hostess in colors to match her table cloth!

Egyptian women wore very wide bracelets on their forearms but no rings. However, they painted their nails and toe nails. Working class women who could not afford real jewelry had imitation jewelry tattooed on their arms and legs.

Scales of bone and metal were used to protect warriors and archers. Gloves have been found that were decorated with bone scales to protect the fingers. The same motifs in bone and metal appear on the leather tunics worn by some pharaohs when they went to war.

Men and women wore the same shoe, a plaited leather sandal, but priests wore sandals made of papyrus reeds. This footwear was fastened by a strap going around the big toe or by thongs running between the first and second toes, then crossed over the arch of the foot and tied to another thong attached to the heel. They were sometimes sewn with beads or decorated with pieces of colored leather.

The robes worn for religious ceremonies resembled those of the pharaohs. But for the more important occasions, the high-priests added an indispensable symbol of their authority: a leopard skin thrown across the right shoulder, with the head of the animal falling waist level. This was the last vestige of mesolithic primitiveness.

Feminine wiles from ancient Egypt - and Europe (left to right) :

One of Nefertiti's daughters tucked her hair in a pearl-studded net. (Louvre Museum.)

Adorning a dancing girl was a lengthy affair.

Princess Semenkare wore a very transparent robe of starched muslin. (1350 B.C. Berlin Museum.)

Elegant women in 1825 did not hesitate to dampen their dresses in order to better reveal the shapes of their bodies. (Bibliothèque Nationale.)

" The sweetest life is to think of nothing."

Sophocles

*"This raven-black hair, glossy
and abundant,
naturally curled..."* Edgar Allan Poe

THE THIRD REVOLUTION

CRETAN CREATIVITY

The island of Crete was first inhabited, in about 3000 B.C., by peasants and shepherds who had come from the Cyclades. They wore chasubles and ponchos cut out of roughly-shaven animal skins. For a long period of time, more than five centuries, this little island slumbered, isolated from all communication with continental Greece and Asia Minor. Then the miracle happened. Travellers from Babylon and Egypt landed on its peaceful shores, playing the role of a Prince Charming in the palace of a Sleeping Beauty. Crete awoke and its population suddenly displayed astonishing creative activity whose products we still admire today.

It is hard to tell whether this upsurge of Cretan civilization was a result of the travellers imposing their tastes and aesthetic standards upon these island folk or whether the innate art of the Cretans developed upon contact with their techniques and ideas. Whatever the reason for the result, this vital and gay people certainly welcomed the new influences with great enthusiasm.

After 2400 B.C., Cretan women started to lengthen their petticoat-like *pagnes*, and slipped a long dagger into their belts. It is interesting to note that this same fashion existed in Denmark during the Bronze Age, but with the difference that the Danes concealed comb beneath the dagger. What will coquetry inspire next...

A close study of Cretan fashions provides us with the surprising observation that this island contained, in embryo form, all the different fashion styles invent-

ed throughout the centuries. The *pagne's* resemblance to a mini-skirt is scarcely worth commenting on, so easy is the comparison. The dress worn by Roman slave-girls can also be evoked. But the earliest model of a skirt such as is depicted on seals dating from the third era of Ancient Minoa reminds one of those worn by our own ladies of fashion in 1823. Gathered in at the waist, it falls to the ground in a bellshape.

Cretan beauties showed considerable taste and imagination where decorative details were concerned. They sewed embroidered strips along the hem which looked so stiff around the full belled skirt that they seem to have been stretched over cane or metal slats, unless they were simply starched or supported by braid sewn crosswise on the inside of the dress. We are irresistibly reminded of the farthingales worn by the none too virtuous ladies of the 14th century and later of the crinolines of the Second Empire.

These insatiable coquettes also decorated their skirts with flounces sewn from top to bottom. Sometimes they were of even width, but when they exceeded a dozen, the widths were graduated. Pleating was also used in a variety of ways as well as lively embroidery: animals real or imaginary, flowers, colored strips and geometrical designs. Once more, we are reminded of the frilled gowns of 1926 and the brightly colored prints worn after the war.

Over these very elaborate models, Cretan ladies sometimes wore sleeveless boleros or long fitted capes.

The bodice, at the Court of Cnossus, was open to the waist in front. This Middle Minoan Era style, of around 2100 B.C. was picked up by Jacques Fath in 1938, albeit somewhat more discretely. The Cretans cut the back of the bodice high on the nape of the

neck like a Medici collar. As for the squeezed-in waist, it reminds us of Marcel Rochas' wasp-waist. Little by little, the collar was to disappear. The bodice remained laced beneath the bosom as in the Middle Ages, covered for gala occasions by a transparent smock like those appearing on illuminated manuscripts and in Italian and Flemish paintings of the 14th century. The sleeves alone remained short, clinging and puffed, like the "leg o' mutton" style of the Renaissance. However they appear to have been attached at the neck and down the back with ribbons or crossed straps.

The World's First Corset...

One of the most striking features of the Cretan costume was undoubtedly the corset... probably the first in the world. It is amusing to imagine what would have happened if Mademoiselle Chanel had been high priestess of fashion at that time, and had thrown her usual curse on this article of clothing so contrary to the freedom of the body. Doubtless, these delightful little mannequins of Antiquity would have been lost to us. The rigidness of this undergarment was probably achieved by the use of copper ribs. It clung to the hips, slimmed the waist and gave a curve to the small bare breasts.

...And High-Heeled Shoes.

For shopping sprees in town, these ladies wore sandals, high-heeled shoes and little high-boots like those worn in 1880. At home however, they walked around barefooted like the men. The latter, for outdoor wear, sported knee-length boots made of white, buff or bright red leather laced several times around

Cretan-style elegance (left to right) :

A casket bearer from a Tirynth fresco. (National Museum, Athens.)

A dress of 1863. (Carnavalet Museum.)

Cretan ladies underlined both eyes and eyebrows. Hair was inventively curled. Several tiers of necklaces and bracelets adorned neck and arms. (Minoan fresco 1500 B.C.)

the leg. But for ceremonial occasions, they wore elegant sandals decorated with beads and tied then at the ankle.

Bermuda shorts were yet another Cretan invention. This surprising innovation was spied on a fresco depicting a lady athlete wearing this type of clinging shorts. This under-garment must have enabled her to accomplish any movement without the risk of indecency, although nudity was scarcely a crime in this period. We can well imagine this young Cretan lady, small, slim, long slender limbs, graceful and vivacious, feminine as one could wish. She is always shown with white skin compared to the men's bronze complexion. She seldom went out yet played a leading role in society, and was not subjected to the bondage of the harem. All the ladies spun and wove wool and flax. The queen herself must have spent her leisure time in this way for a distaff is reproduced on the door of her apartment in the palace of Cnossus. The dyes in use were subtle and varied, and were obtained from vegetable extracts. Purple dye came from the shells of that famous little whelk whose lovely red color the Phoenicians were the first to use and to exploit commercially on a large scale.

With such a wealth of ideas, it is not surprising that for more than three centuries Cretan fashion was adopted by the majority of the countries bordering the Black Sea and the Eastern Mediterranean. Intact from the 18th century B.C. right up to 1450 B.C. the power of the kings of Cnossus and the unbridled taste on the part of persons of high rank for clothing and jewelry had turned this small court into a veritable pole of attraction for the entire Near East. Where dresses were concerned the most extraordinary variety of forms and trimmings appeared during the last Minoan Era between 1580 and 1450 B.C. Women seemed to be mainly concerned with elegance and pureness of line, yet they wore a padded belt which they tied over the navel and which does not seem to be particularly attractive to us. On the other hand their hats — and what hats — were incredible; round, flat, bonnet-shaped, tiaras, berets, truncated cones, upturned cornets, draped, ornamented with rosettes, feathers and ribbons. Here we find the predecessors of the 1830 cabriolets, the 1920 turbans and the many fancy shapes produced by Fath, Dior or Balenciaga over the last thirty years or so. The headgear of one young lady however leaves us quite perplexed. Her head is wrapped in wavy bands topped by a high bonnet similar to those worn by a modern-day chef.

These ladies of Crete had, it seems, a taste for diadems and for crowns made of leaves or plaques of gold. They also fancied hairpins made of gold or copper and ornamented with rock crystals, quartz, animal heads or flowers.

The men, less ostentatious, walked about bare-chested wearing *pagnes* of various shapes and fabrics. Made of linen or wool, and sometimes of leather, the *pagnes* were draped to form a double apron often with a kind of tapering point at the back, a style reminiscent of prehistoric man's need to wear an

(left to right) :

The beauty of the Greek drapé is seen in this detail from a kylix picturing the rape of Helen. (early 5th century B.C., British Museum.)

The Greek sandal used for walking in town. (530 B.C., Louvre Museum.)

The buskin was worn in France between 1795 and 1799, during the Directory regime. (Bibliothèque Nationale, Paris.)

animal skin knotted around his waist as a sign of power. The Cretan *pagne* was held up by a belt designed to emphasize the slimness of the waist. Male Cretans must have been vain indeed about their silhouette to go to such lengths. The belts were often decorated with spirals or rosettes made of gold, silver or copper.

As protection against the rain and the cold, they wore a long coat made either of an animal skin or of thick wool. Priests wore capes during ceremonies which were covered with scales or heavy embroideries while kings and princes wore long tunics of richly colored fabrics. Shoes were used only for outdoor wear.

THE FOURTH REVOLUTION

THE GREEK DRAPE

The Greeks despite their familiarity with the styles worn by the Mesopotamians, and with the refinements invented by the Egyptians and the Cretans, settled for a steady diet of draped costumes, which seem, at first glance, to be highly monotonous.
According to Leon Heuzey, the French authority on classic fashions, " The draped costume was never fitted, either tailored or cut but was composed of a single rectangular piece of cloth, the length of which varied according to its use as a tunic or a coat... "
But upon examining closely the metopes of Olympus or the friezes of the Parthenon, it becomes immediately apparent that this drapery possessed an infinite variety of styles depending on whether or not it was worn with a belt, was short or long, thrown over the arm or across the shoulders.

Originally, during the third millennium, those Greeks living along the Aegean Sea wore the *pagne*, the prehistoric mini-dress. Theirs was made of roughly woven wool. A thousand years later, the first Aryan migrations pushed the Achaians to invade Greece and the primitive costume lengthened its hemline. Eight centuries later the Dorians, a mountain people, drove out the Achaians and appeared before their new subjects garbed in woolen coats embellished with a hood. The Greeks who often shivered in the heart of winter gratefully adopted this extra garment.

Linen first imported in to Greece by the Ionians brought about a considerable change in the draped costume by making it much lighter. Weaving was also greatly improved thanks to techniques brought in from Egypt and Mesopotamia.
Herodotus tells us that linen tunics were imposed upon the women of Athens by their husbands, annoyed by their stabbing with their mantle clasps the last survivor of the Battle of Aegina in 558 B.C. But perhaps jealousy caused their anger for the peplum worn by their women was slit up the side to reveal the thighs clear to the waist.

In time this garment was fastened on both shoulders and sewn down either side. Resembling a shirt, this *khiton* was caught at the waist at two levels so as to allow a fullness in between. At night it fell straight.

Twelve centuries before the birth of Christ, baths were common. However women were not permitted to use them nor were children who had to stand up in a tub and be doused by hot water poured over them by slaves. The men however bathed in bathtubs made of earthenware, polished stone or solid silver. Later these appliances were replaced by bathing pools supplied with water run in through a pipe.
Without doubt ancient Greece was one of the temples of the world in which beauty and grace were worshipped on an equal footing with the goddesses. But from the 4th century on, the power of the courtesans entailed a slackening of morals and taste. Fashions remained the same but lewdness and luxury and a desire to show off one's possessions heralded the wind of change, sweeping away the temperance that had been displayed up until then.

The most surprising description of the care which a rich courtesan gave herself is to be found in the *Corinthian Nights:* " Her slaves massaged her from head to foot before placing her in a scented bath; she was then caressed with swan's feathers so as to dry the parts of her body which were still damp. Then, she was rubbed with perfumed oils brought from the Orient. A depilatory was then carefully applied. Her hair was washed, perfumed and pomaded before being plaited. Her coiffure was completed with filigree braid, gold and silver lame ribbons. A black coating touched up her eyebrows and the edges of her eyelids were touched with a brush dipped in incense black. Her eyes were widened with lines of kohl. " Beauty masks were composed mainly of white of ceruse which concealed for a few hours lines and other small imperfections but removed all natural coloring. To touch up their cheeks, women used *purpurissium* made from a root imported from Syria and macerated in vinegar. Teeth were cleaned with brushes dipped in aromatic powder, and the tongue scraped with an ivory blade. The beautiful courtesan kept a fragrant liquor in her mouth for a time in order to refresh and perfume her breath. The Greeks held the hair of their wives in such high esteem that they would even swear on it. A tress of hair given as a token of love was revered as a relic by the lover. But a jealous man who had reason to doubt the fidelity of his love did not hesitate to shave her head in order to keep her from going out. When in mourning, elegant women colored their hair ebony black... When all was well, they dyed it blonde " like the Attic cloud " or powdered gold, silver white or red. Women generally preferred to be blonde, and lightened their natural color by rinsing it in a potassium solution and rubbing it with a pomade of yellow flowers.

The grace of women in ancient Greece (left to right) :

A statuette from Tanagra shows a draped costume of 330 B.C. (British Museum.)

A young Spartan girl is portrayed in bronze. (End. of 6th century B.C., British Museum.)

Aphrodite was also created in bronze. (5th century B.C., Louvre Museum.)

Variations on the drapery theme are shown here in details drawn from Greek vases.
(left to right pgs 26-27):

Lady with a flower is from a kylix discovered at Vulci.

Flute-player and dancing girl figure on a kylix discovered at Vulci.

A farewell scene is on a kylix found at Capua.

A pilgrim with leopard comes from a kylix discovered at Vulci. (5th century B.C., the above, British Museum.)

The flute-player was taken from an Italian krater of about 410 B.C. (Tarentum Museum, Italy.)

The Roman version of the drapé is seen here (left to right):

A bronze statuette portrays a woman in a hooded cape. (Saint-Germain-en-Laye Museum.)

An aristocratic lady dining appears on a fresco. (Rome)

This portrait of a lady figures in a fresco in the Villa of Mysteries.

According to certain statues of 6th century B.C. goddesses wore a coiffure of bands of hair "tiered and waved with curling irons" or decorated with metal spirals. Men and women alike loved wigs to which they gave different names to designate their use. The *entrikhton* was intended for bald patches; the *procomion* was worn like a crown and the *penike* as a toupee. Needles for unravelling hair and curling irons were to be found on all dressing tables. But, as Lucien, a Greek author of the 2nd century A.D. wrote, "If one could see women getting out of bed, one would find them even less attractive than monkeys." Thus the motivation for all the artifices.

Athens exerted a great influence on Rome through the Imperial officials who dressed in the Oriental fashion while visiting Greece and continued wearing the *peplos* when they returned home. They also brought back the taste for luxury, jewelry and perfume. In Rome, several types of dress were used by men as well as women. The latter however wore a brassière called a *mamillare* which they wore with their *pagne-panty*. A kind of shirt called the *subucula* was worn under the *tunica* or informal dress, and constitutes the birth of women's lingerie.

" *A woman is always in the situation which she imposes as a result of the illusion which she knows so well how to produce.*"

Guy de Maupassant

Two variations of the drapé in Roman times (left to right):

A lady of high Neapolitan aristocracy. (Naples Museum.)

These Roman sculptures from Villa of the Papiri in Herculanum were inspired by Greek models of the 5th century B.C. As the ladies walked, the Greek peplum, which was open down the side, revealed their thighs right up to the waist... or nearly so. Little wonder that Athenian husbands forced their wives to wear the "kiton", a kind of chemise gathered at the waist, as early as the middle of the 6th cen. B.C.

The ceremonial dress or *stola* was floor length, had sleeves and was tied beneath the breasts with a cord. A wide belt bound the waist, raising the skirt slightly so as to reveal the tip of the foot.

A kind of train known as the *insita* was allowed to trail behind in the style dear to 1880.

Patrician Roman women often wore over this *stola* a short tunic with silken sleeves ornamented with golden tassels. A *pallium*, or coat, was draped around the shoulder without clasp or brooch. The ladies also carried a complex paraphernalia: hankies, fans and parasols.

Matrons of this era were idle beyond words. They used their income and their slaves in order to adorn themselves and to preserve their beauty. Certain of them used, even in front of their husbands, beauty masks that were called "the husband's mask".

They dyed their hair blond or a blazing auburn through the use of a soap made by the Germans according to a Gallic formula. This dye was then rolled into balls and sent to the perfumers in Rome. These same Germans also exported large quantities of human hair which the Roman market absorbed completely.

Roman brides wore saffron colored coats and sandals of the same color. Their coiffure which was topped by six false curls, was covered by a flame-colored veil, the *flammeum*, and a crown of flowers, usually of sweet marjoram and verbena. Myrtle and orange-blossoms were preferred. Our present day brides are direct descendants of the Roman virgins.

Romans living during the last centuries before our era wore short Etruscan togas similar to the Greek *chlamydes* but narrow and clinging tightly to the shoulders. Later this toga was widened, so much so that the wearer would have difficulty in draping it without help. It was wound about the wearer so that the fullness formed a pouch in front.

During the 2nd century A.D., Romans of the lower classes gave up the long toga in favor of the greek-inspired *pallium*, a more practical garment which was worn over the short Gallic *sagum*.

Men spent hours over their toilet. Their hairdressers known as *tonsores* curled their hair with little tongs. These gentlemen also used make-up and went so far as to apply beauty-patches and use perfume extravagantly. The length of beards varied at different times. In the 2nd century B.C., they disappeared altogether only to reappear under the influence of Emperor Hadrian.

There were many variations of hats. The *galerus* which fitted tightly around the head was perhaps the forerunner of the " galurin " worn by our grandmothers. The *petasus* of Greek origin which can be seen on so many figurines had a wide brim and a crown which varied in height and shape. The most typical came from Anatolia.

Sandals were attached by high-laced thongs but peasants wore ankle-laced boots, the sole reinforced with iron.

HENNIN
AND
POLISH LEATHERS

" God's servants are none but jugglers who must raise men's hearts and fill them with spiritual joys"   *Francis of Assisi*

Medieval costumes reflected their wearers' role in society (left to right):

Louis I of Anjou, King of Sicily, in the uniform of the Order of the Holy Ghost (1352). He wears a metalwork belt from which hangs a long ceremonial sword. Normally, the belt would be used for hanging a pouch-shaped purse and a dagger then called the "gazelaire".

A Knight of the Order of the Holy Ghost, hooded and with a gold insignia on his breast.

A female juggler and musician. (Bibliothèque Nationale, Paris.)

THE FIFTH REVOLUTION

GALLIC INNOVATIONS

Gaul, before its conquest by the Romans, knew little of luxury. The people lived like savages. But in less than a century, everything was to change. The ladies of Gaul, impressed by the splendors of the Romans, began to care for their personal appearance. Following the example of Roman matrons, they began to use cosmetics and to tint their eyelashes with soot. They washed their faces with beer foam and covered their cheeks with vermilion as well as with a paste composed of chalk dissolved in vinegar.

Madame Gauloise was most proud of her hair. When its color was too dark, she tinted it with a paste made of cinders and horse fat which made her hair glow with deep red tints. This combination plus soda was, according to Pliny, the origin of soap.

On festival days, her hair was caught on the top of her head in a crest and woven with threads of gold or powdered with finely sieved white cinders.

In the days when Gaul was becoming a roman province, aqueducts and thermal baths sprang up in all the developing cities. The rarety of lingerie made bathing indispensable but at the same time, it was a sign of poverty rather than opulence. The bather had to wash himself and his clothes at the same time. Later, as the Saxons, Burgundians and Franks began their series of invasions in the 5th century and occupied one after the other the provinces of Gaul. the women lost their taste for make-up. " Asceti

Of the falconer or his bird of prey,
which has the most piercing eyes?

cism " became fashionable and no one would dream of painting her face. " The Gauls, " Ammien Marcellin, a chronicler of the day wrote, " were always properly dressed, carefully groomed and washed. " In the 10th century, two tunics were worn, one atop the other. The " *chainse* ", the ancestor of our shirt, was made of white linen while the other, the " *bliaud* " came down to the knees and was made of wool or silk... Shortly before the time of the Capetians in 987 A.D., it was fashionable to tuck the latter into the *braies* or breeches as we tuck a shirt into trousers. Subsequently, it was slightly pulled out of the belt so as to allow a fullness both at the back and the front. The coat then popular was short and made of a striped, flowered or checkered material.

Refined people attached their shoes with luxuriously made garters, often multicolored, the ends of which dangled freely.

Shoes which were very narrow became longer and ended in an up-turned toe toward the end of the 10th century. Clothes continued to be decorated with colored braid as in the days of the Romans and French nobility hung gold coins on the hems of their tunics... the first signs of ostentation.

Henry II, Emperor of Germany, was the first to wear a pocket on his white silk-damask bliaud. Hemmed with wide strips of violet-blue brocaded silk and green silk piping, this new item with its vertical opening appeared just below the neckline near the heart. Tinkers and other artisans had no such refinement as a pocket and went about surrounded by an assortment of objects which dangled from straps on all sides: hammer, pincers, tinder-box, touch-wood etc. In those days, furs were the most luxurious item of all and were considered by the feudal lords to be the very symbol of opulence, rather like the Rolls or the Bentley today. They covered themselves in ermine, called the " skin of Babylon ", in sable, in Northern squirrel which was worked in an alternating pattern of squares back and front called " little vair " and " big vair " depending on the size of the squares, and in black and white fox from the Caspian sea. These skins cost a fortune. However, their success was such that those who could not afford such sumptuous peltry fell back on skins such as lamb, hare, cat and even dog ! Indeed, furs were so indispensable that they were even included amongst the clothes distributed to the poor.

Certain skins were dyed, mainly in red. Saint Bernard was shocked by " the crimson fur cuffs " displayed by some of the cardinals. These trimmings were known as "gules", hence the name given to the red color on coats of arms. They even went so far as to make striped coats, using different colored strips of fur ! This was the period during which " flecked " ermine first became fashionable.

Women also wore the bliaud, but it was ankle-length. Its funnel-shaped sleeves revealed the sleeves of the chainse beautifully puffed or trimmed with fine gold braid.

Another garment known as the " gipe " or " gypoun " a word used until the 18th century to signify jerkin, was tightly fitted to the bust so as to outline its shape, and hooked down the side. The coat was attached over the breast with a wide clasp of wrought metal.

Feminine hair-styles were romantic in the extreme: the hair was parted in the middle and gathered into two plaits interlaced with ribbons. On the forehead, a string of beads, a guirlande or else a circle of wrought gold was placed. Coquetry became more widespread and Guibert of Nogent, French Benedictine historian, describing the beautiful ladies of the period, wrote: " Not one of them, but would feel

(left to right) :

A scout explains to William the Conqueror the movements of Harold II before the battle of Hastings. (Bàyeux Museum.)

A man nursing a falcon.

A Carolingian figure. (Bibliothèque Nationale.)

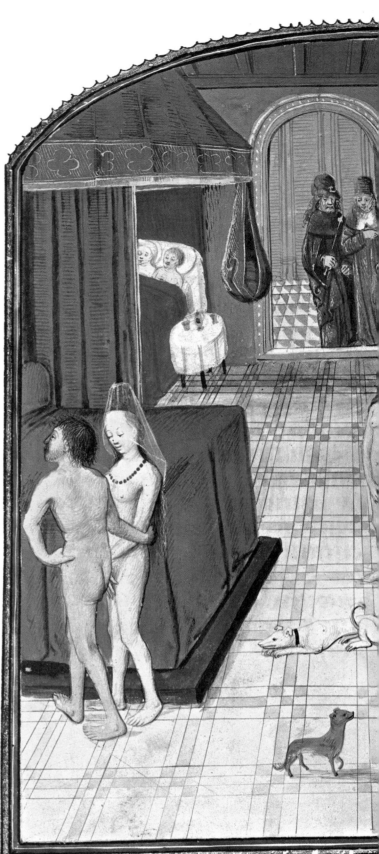

herself to be the most miserable of creatures if she were to be without a circle of admirers. " This was a remarkable reversal of the traditional attitude toward women as Guibert noted. " They were ", he wrote, "sworn at in the coarsest manner, dragged by the hair and threatened with the sword or the stick for a look or a smile. " The Salic Law, which prevailed between the 6th and the 13th centuries punished " the act of touching a free woman's arm " with a fine of 25 gold sous... twice as much as the rape of a slavegirl, but no more than the theft of a bull. "But suddenly they have become an object of perpetual adoration ", noted the surprised chronicler. " The bravest warriors tremble before them." Starting with the 10th century, economic considerations took on considerable importance in the development of European costume. Sea communication between the Orient and the West was reestablished, bringing with it a thousand sources for clothing luxury. The emperors of Byzantium exported brightly colored cloths, of a lightness and richness unknown up to that time, — such as the taffeta called " cendal "— which arrived in Italy via Venice. Silken cloths, woven in Andalousia, became fashionable in France as a result of the Arab occupation of Spain.

Silk brocade from Egypt, known as *Alexandrine paile* also made its appearance, as well as a purple-dyed silk cloth called *osterin*, together with a cloth called *siglaton* made in the Cyclades etc... In the North, weavers mainly produced a cotton, called *fustian*, and a muslin, called *mollequin*. Enormous quantities of sheets were produced in Flanders, Picardy, Champagne and Languedoc. The French speciality was a horizontally-striped cloth with several colors repeated at wide intervals.

Medieval manners (left to right) :

A man loses his hose in this detail of a manuscript.

In the 13th century, the public baths were sometimes turned into parlours of... chance acquaintance, where everyone made merry. Hats were kept on, but virtue was cast aside. "Cosy little suppers" were served by maidens clothed only in their charms.

Sweating-baths were popular and public in the 15th century (miniature).

A French village scene in the 16th century; breeches secured by cords can be seen at left and also the women's bonnets which have scarcely changed through the centuries (Bibliothèque Nationale.)

The Byzantines contributed an enamelling process formerly employed in Roman Gaul and now perfected. Throughout Europe, out-sized clasps of great beauty, used for fastening coats, belts made up of plaques and stone-set rings were chased in gold and silver.

After the Second Crusade, Europe developed a taste for luxury and pleasure. The Crusaders brought back not only a new sense of refinement, but also a desire for more ample and longer clothes.

A small sensation occurred when men, who had shaved ever since the Roman conquest, began to grow beards. One of the obvious reasons, it seems, for this lengthening of hair and bristle was the great " terror " of the year 1000. The expected end of the world drove poor human beings to a closer contact with nature so as to be better prepared for the ascent to Heaven... It seemed more sensible, indeed, to appear before one's Maker in a more natural state... true to the principles of Saint Paul who wrote in his Epistle to the Corinthians: "Does not Nature herself teach us that it is shameful for man to care for his hair." The word "care for" can, however, be understood in two different ways: to cut and trim, or on the contrary, to grow and care for. Hair-styles also changed; the head was shaven in front and hair long at the back. This cut was attributed to Constance, daughter of the Count of Arles, who imposed this Provençal fashion at the Court of France when she got married, in 1003, to Robert the Pious.

Some gentlemen, by way of a reaction, allowed their

" No man spits on his own beard." (German proverb)

Captions from left to right:

Hoods of different styles from a 14th century manuscript. (Bibliothèque Nationale.)

A bronze candle-bearer.

Candle-bearer holding two goblets. (Cluny Museum.)

hair to grow in front, shaved the backs of their necks and added an unexpected ornament: a thick curl coiled onto the forehead and known as the " dorelot " whence the French word "dorloter" meaning to mollycoddle. The Church protested against these fashions because one could no longer differentiate between pilgrims and " men of means ". Bishops even went so far as to refuse to give the Sacrament to the faithful who kept their hair long. They forced sinners to have themselves shorn and shaven if they wished to be forgiven their wrongs.

But the habit had been acquired and men continued to curl their hair in the napes of their necks or to gather it up into a bun by means of ribbons, or rosaries or " hair-nets " studded with pearls and stones and knotted around their heads. They even parted their beards into small tufts which they ornamented with golden threads.

Women also changed their hair-style. Tresses were replaced by flattened hair surrounded by a roll held in place with narrow bands and pins with big carved heads.

Smart women dyed their hair blond or black, but never red which symbolized wickedness. They used depilatory creams, soothing ointments, powders, toothpastes and rubbed their cheeks.

Fashion required that they cover their heads with a cloth which shrouded their necks and the tops of their shoulders. The end was allowed to hang down on their left arms. This veil was known as a " wimple ".

Women —and sometimes even men— wore flowered hats when they went out. A sort of coronet, it was made of cornflowers, roses or fresh violets during the summer season and of leaves during the winter. This led to the formation of a new corporation of flower-gardeners specialized in hair-styling. Other hats were made of a moulded form covered with satin, velvet or taffeta and decorated with embroidery, braid or plumes. Beneath it; a veil was wrapped

(From left to right) :

A French physician prescribes a leek as a remedy. During Charles V's reign, elegant women wore their headdresses padded in the shapes of hearts, trefoils, pointed horns or rounded coifs. These were called "attires". (Bibliothèque Nationale, Paris.)

This young Flemish woman wears a rolled ribbon headdress trimmed with fringes. Part of a triptych, it belongs to the Braque family, circa 1500, and was painted by Van Eyck. (Louvre Museum.)

" When a woman has the gift of holding her tongue,

she merits that the highest praise of her be sung."

Corneille

Hats, hoods and coifs hid hairdos in the Middle Ages (left to right):

In the mid-14th century it was fashionable to wear "truffles". Hair was plaited or rolled over metal frames and topped by a starched veil which hung gracefully down to the shoulders as seen in this painting of a family meal.

The sleeves of men's jackets no longer extend beyond elbow length, but have flaps hanging to the knees. Belts are worn over the thighs. The cowl-shaped hood finishes in a point behind. (Bibliothèque Nationale.)

Mary of Saux has a squared frame on her coif.

Jeanne of Budes, a native of Brittany wears a draped version.

Marguerite la Gervine, wife of Jacques the Bourgeois, wore a hooded covering.

Françoise Auve, wife of Yvon Pierre, Knight, Lord of Bellefontaine in Anjou, preferred a lampshade form.

Peasants wore oriental-style hats. (Bibliothèque Nationale.)

tightly around the hair and knotted beneath the chin in the manner of motorists in 1900.

Medieval beauties also wore *chaperons*, a kind of hood, with rounded cap. Later, it extended down the back of the neck. Cowls of cloth or velvet lined with fur, known as *amices*, were also popular.

Men wore a similar *chaperon* topped by a hat with a spiked crown made of cotton, woollen or hairfelt, and trimmed with fur in winter. The last word in smartness was the peacock hat covered with the eyes of the feathers stuck onto the felt. Men often wore their hair hidden beneath a white bonnet tied under the chin. Dandies had these bonnets cut out of cambric and decorated them with bouquets or little birds... This fashion lasted nearly two centuries. When " Mother Nature " had been ungenerous, men and women wore wigs made of " dead " hair. Hair cut from living people's heads was not used at that time. This brought forth more protests from the Church against the Christians who were accused of wearing hair " whose owners were perhaps roasting in Hell. "

Both sexes made great use of perfumes, especially musk which was contained in gold or silver spheres called " scent apples ", perforated with small holes. The most revolutionary change of all occurred when male clothing, which had been worn short (midcalf) for six hundred years, suddenly lengthened. This fashion is said to have been launched by Robert Short-Hose, Duke of Normandy, after a trip to Sicily

where he had gone with a group of loose-living princes to meet some of his former compatriots. He decided there and then that all the young men among his followers should dress " in the manner of women ": with their hair hanging down to the napes of their necks and clothes trailing along the ground. During the reign of Philip Augustus, the German fashion consisting of tails cut at the bottom of the overcoat was adopted in France. It was soon replaced by a style which required this garment to be opened in front and at either side. Long " wings " also appeared behind the arms as well as short, wide-open sleeves. This style was called the " bold-coat ". Beneath, the breeches were attached to the thighs with a cord. The entire outfit, that is to say, tunic, surcoat, bold-coat and cape —sometimes called " dust-sheet "— was known as the " robe ".

In winter, the " necklet " or short mantle was also worn.

The ancestor of the " silent valet " of the 20th century was a pole placed near the bedside on which clothes were piled. It occurred to me that it would be amusing to look up, in a 13th century guide to good manners, how the coat hanger was used.

It is worth remembering that cupboards did not exist at that time and that chests were used for travelling or for putting away best clothes, just as was done in French farmhouses right up to the last century.

" You should ", instructed the guide, " spread out

...*"A woman's duty is to stay at home and hold her peace."*

Plutarch

on the pole your coat, surcoat, cloche-hat, doublet and everything you have in the way of furs and winter and summer clothing. Your shirt and breeches should be kept beneath the bolster of the bed. In the mornings, when you get up, you should first of all put on your shirt and breeches. Then you should put on your braces and your fustian and, after that, your hood. Thereafter, it will be the turn of hose and shoes to be followed by the robes which complete your dress. Finally, you should tighten your straps and wash your hands. "

On reading this, one might be tempted to believe that cleanliness did not play any great part in daily life. Only wealthy people owned the ancestor of the " sauna ", a bell-like sheet covering burning-hot stones onto which water was thrown. Yet baths were often taken " after perspiring in a public sweat-

ing-room ". The public baths rapidly became public meeting places. Contemporary illustrations in psalters, in paintings and engravings show rooms hung with material and fitted with lines of wooden tubs. Men and women, wearing plumed hats, can be seen soaking opposite each other and eating delicacies laid out on a plank between the two rows of tubs. We should add that these rogues were waited upon by maids clothed only in their charms... and generously gifted with bust and rump. A writer of the period confides that: " women enjoyed these baths even more than men and lolled in them in both female and male company ". Some particularly considerate lovers even had soft music played during their bathing ! What a delightful age !

Nevertheless, it was not as free as might be imagined. A notice appeared on the doors of these bathing

Habits and headdresses of the medieval housewife (left to right):

The women in the family of the Founder of the Order of the Knights of the Stag in England are pictured as very devout.

"The Ending of the True Cross" attributed to Simon Marmian in the 15th century contains different styles of padded and horned headdresses.

The halos surrounding mother and child in this 15th century painting recall the Nativity.

The French poet, Christine de Pisan, wears "truffles" with padding on top. (Bibliothèque Nationale.)

45

establishments to the effect that entry was forbidden to "women of ill repute, lepers and tramps".

Although people did not wash much in the mornings, they made much use of scents. In the 14th century, violet was the predominating odour, but the apartments were perfumed with the forerunner of the atomizer, the "cyprus oyselet", a kind of flexible ball which sprinkled a scented powder when squeezed. The first perfume containing alcohol, Hungarian water made of cedar, rosemary, turpentine, was given to Charles V in 1370.

It is believed that mourning, the wearing of black, first began to be worn in France during the reign of Philip the Fair.

The use of black, probably introduced from Spain, seems curious in relation to the customs when the body was surrounded by a spectacular display based on a single color: yellow for the Egyptians (an allusion to withered leaves), grey for the Ethiopians (a reminder of ashes), white for women in both Rome and Sparta, a symbol of purity. Violet came later, being a mixture of red (the color of mourning for royalty) and blue (expressing both sorrow and trust in Heaven). The men of Rome and Sparta however wore black, which symbolized immortality. It is written in Ecclesiastes that mourning should only last seven days for "sadness hastens death and sorrow fetters energy and weakens reason".

Solomon was a wise man. It is very probable that Lycurgus was inspired by these good principles when he limited, four centuries before Christ, the period of mourning in Greece to eleven days. The Romans made it last as much as ten months.

History has it that Mahaut of Artois, in 1303, went into mourning for her husband by wearing black and having her bed and the walls of her room hung in the same color. But it was not, it seems, until the death of John II the Good (1364) that the king's heir dressed in black at the death of his predecessor and remained in mourning until the funeral service. After which, the court remained in mourning whereas the new king wore purple.

In the 15th century, full mourning consisted, for men, of a long black coat and an "overlapping hood" or cowl which was lowered to hide the face.

Mourning was extremely rigorous for women. Eleanor of Poitiers. who was a court lady in the reign of Philip the Good and wrote a book of good manners, described 15th century habits as follows: "I have heard that the Queen of France must remain a whole year without leaving her bed-chamber, the said bed-chamber, as well as the other rooms being hung in black," She added: "As soon as Madame de Charolais learned of the death of her father, she stayed in her room for six weeks, lying all the time on a bed covered with a white sheet. The other princesses have to do the same! but the banneresses (wives of knights) only have to remain nine days on the bed for a father, and during the remainder of the six weeks must sit before their bed on a large black sheet. For a husband, they must remain lying down for six weeks."

*"When a fur-lined coat is warm,
it should be kept in good repair."* Herondas

The all-enveloping styles of the Middle Ages featured (left to right):
sleeves called "mufflers" which splay out and come right down to the fingers.

the ample folds and sleeves of a lady of Navarre.

the pleated cape of a Moorish woman of Grenada. (Bibliothèque Nationale, Paris.)

47

THE SIXTH REVOLUTION

THE END OF THE MIDDLE AGES

At the close of the 13th century, fashion had changed little in the past centuries although a revolution in thought which had begun two hundred years earlier was shaking the world.

Man was learning to control his instincts and was becoming more and more sensitive to refinement and luxury. He sought beauty; woman now became not only a companion to him, but also his source of inspiration.

Christians were still fervent believers, but were less influenced by the demands of a Church which had become dictatorial in its demands for obedience to a rigorous religious regime. The people had discovered the good things of life and now they wanted to indulge in them. It should be remembered that economic conditions had greatly improved despite the Hundred Years War. European trade, forsaking overland routes, had resumed its activity by sea. Ports such as Venice, Genoa, Marseilles and Barcelona to the south, Antwerp and Bruges in the north developed to such an extent that French fashions were to appear as far north as Greenland... though, admittedly, with the help of a Norman colony which had settled there.

And suddenly, throughout Europe, fashion appears to have evolved along parallel lines, in the same way that certain trends sweep through all our fashion houses simultaneously, resulting in the same lengths, the same colors, the same width of shoulders or lack of bosom...

In 1340, for no apparent reason, the long tunic worn

Turbans for men and cones for women (left to right):

Philip the Bold, Duke of Burgundy, was painted wearing a hat rolled into a turban.

Mary, a 15th-century Duchess of Burgundy also wore a surcoat of flecked ermine.

The two young people in a 16th-century flower garden wear the same styles as their elders.
(Bibliothèque Nationale.)

by men was replaced in France, Italy and England by a narrow garment called a " jacket ". The garment worn beneath this —the " doublet " or " gypoun ", as it was called— was padded. Hose, the forerunner of our stockings, crept upwards to mould the calves and thighs and were attached to the lining of the doublet, while the breeches which had been full-sized trousers in Gallic times, shrank to the point where they were no bigger than drawers. Clothes had become tight-fitting.

At this point, the question arises: where had this short fashion —which was to be adopted by all the elegant men in Europe— come from ? Undoubtedly from Italy where women's praises had long been sought and where men to impress the fair sex went to such lengths that one might easily be watching the love-dance of birds of paradise.

It is not surprising, therefore, that the first fashion designers should have made their appearance in the land of Dante. What imagination and richness a designer such as Pisanello displayed when he worked at a court costume ! It must be said that the Italians, who were optimists by nature and enjoyed extraordinary economic prosperity despite constant political upheavals, had a marked preference for colors, for striking brocades and shimmering silks. It is amusing to note that noblemen of the 14th and 15th centuries decorated their sleeves, especially the right hand one, with " badges " of the period: insignia, emblems, escutcheons etc... in order to recognize each other.

Sleeves were extravagant. One known as a " train " which was attached with ribbons or laces to the shoulder or elbow, was tightly fitted and buttoned as far as the elbow and extended down to the first finger-joint like a " mitten ". Both sexes also wore " sewn sleeves " which were tacked unto the garment in the morning and taken off at night. On the occasion of a particularly brilliant tournament, enraptured women were seen to throw down their sleeves to the victors just as they throw their shoes nowadays into the arena at a bull fight. Sentimental women often offered their sleeves to their beloved.

The men, in an attempt to display originality, wore a different stocking on each leg, one striped and the other black. In Venice, men even went so far as to spangle one of their hose with precious stones ! In England, the young lords, " independent " as ever, flaunted a loud eccentricity by wearing coats and hose of different colors. Nor did they hesitate to cover themselves with jewelry like women.

Spain, torn with internal strife between the provinces of Aragon and Castille, took longer to stabilize her politics and riches. Furthermore, the austerity of her customs and her rigid Catholicism favored neither ostentation nor extravagant fashions.

The German Empire, in the process of splitting up into states, lived in an atmosphere of civil war and should not have been thinking of either luxury or originality. Yet it was here that a strange fashion called " lead tatters " was invented. The hems of dresses, coats, sleeves and even headgear were

shredded like a built-in fringe. This idea was a new one and was immediately copied in France after being adopted by the Dukes of Burgundy who were always on the look-out for new eccentricities. They did not hesitate to tighten and shorten their doublets to the utmost, a trend which inspired the author of the *chronique de Saint-Denis,* to write: " Some had costumes so short that they reached only to their buttocks and so tight that help was required to put them on and it seemed as though they were being skinned when taking them off. Others wore robes flounced over their hips like women and even had their hose of one color on one leg and of another on the other. "
As for Philip of Mézières, the philosopher, he blamed the doublet for upsetting digestion, so tightly did it press upon the stomach. Costumes were also worn which were entirely pierced with cut-outs in the shape of stars and through which could be spied the different color of the dress beneath. Clothes were " shredded ", marbled, butterflied.
At the close of the 12th century, shoes were of leather, wax-polished, decorated with braid or colored embroidery and with the ends turned up, inspired by the Orient, as mentioned earlier. These pointed ends were called " pistachios ". Indoor shoes, cut

low and open, were the ancestors of our present-day pumps.
Women enjoyed being entertained by the sweet nothings of minstrels, and frequented " love courts ". They drew from the novels of the time a thousand sources of inspiration for their charms and flirtations. To have wasp-waists, they choked themselves with embroidered belts decorated with golden plaques sometimes weighing more than $2\frac{1}{2}$ lbs. They hitched up their skirts so as to reveal the tips of their toes and discovered " hip suppleness ". Coquettes of the day were swinging their hips.
Court nobility revolved around the sovereigns. The rich gentry looked for ways to imitate the nobles and economic prosperity added its weight to this expansion as well as to the artistic and intellectual renewal of all Europe.
One of the characteristic features of the period was the predominance of silk over linen. Although the " spider-web " of Ypres and the " stripes " of Gand were still used, velvet and brocaded silk were now all the rage.
And the height of luxury ? Ostrich feathers, which cost a small fortune. As for pearls, these were used on hats, belts, doublets, shoes and even on coats of

The more the girls are young and fair, the higher the stove-pipes they wear.

armor ! The Duke of Bourbon's armor had no less than six hundred of them... as well as rubies and sapphires ! As a result, the tears shed by oysters also increased in unbelievable proportions.

Shoes, boots and " soled " hose extended beyond the toe to such a point that it had to be reinforced with whale-bones. This shape, which had come from the Orient, had taken hold in Poland before arriving in France where it was called " Polish leathers ".

The toes of these Polish slippers flapped on the ground when one walked, to such an extent that certain young blades attached the points of these shoes with small gold or silver chains to a spot below the knee.

An edict issued by Charles V condemned this fashion as a " deformity thought up as a mockery of God and His Holy Church. "

A strange custom consisted in wearing a single yellow boot, a fashion which was adopted by the fair sex. Some ungallant young blades accused these ladies of having taken over male prerogatives and took their case to the poet Martial d'Auvergne who dismissed their claim. But not all medieval manhood was so defiant. Knights on horseback lived up to the traditions of chivalry. They took the lady of their dreams for an outing with them by slipping a lock of her hair into the woven bridles of their mounts. When we marvel nowadays at certain of the disguises worn by our precious young things, we need only refer back to the 14th century to realize that in the course of every fashion revolution, youth has delighted in startling the crowds. The young men of those days lengthened the linings of their hoods —which were already monumental— until the ends were flapping against their calves " like animal's tails ". They also cut their hair, trimmed their beards " Spanish style " and allowed their moustaches to hang down. The most amusing part about it was that their fathers began (just as they do today) by crying shame, and then, finding this a pretext for growing young again... they followed their sons' example !

The fair sex was greatly preoccupied with hair-styles. Plaits were hitched up so as to hang in front of the ears down to throat level. The rest of the hair was entwined around the head and covered with a starched veil. On top of this was placed a hood which was sometimes very pointed.

This style was soon replaced by " truffles ", locks

(left to right):

A portrait of a woman by Van der Weyden. (National Portrait Gallery.)

The variety of the fringed coifs and truffles bears witness to the exquisite refinement of the court of the Duchy of Burgundy. The uniformly white color of the dresses and costumes seems to indicate that this is a reception with an imposed theme. The Duke of Burgundy wears "Polish leather" pattens. Most of the other men wear soled hose. (Versailles Museum.)

of hair rolled or braided onto metal mountings which held them over the ears. These were covered by cambric on which was placed a draped fabric covering both neck and chin, a bonnet still worn today by certain orders of nuns.

Hair, having fallen from favor, was concealed beneath fringed head-dresses decorated with pearl diadems, or " gold hats " worked in metal. In the reign of Charles V, the head-dress was surrounded by pads which were arranged in front in the shape of hearts, trefoils or up-turned or flattened horns.

We are amused when Marie-Antoinette's hairdresser, Léonard, tries to take credit for such fantasies as the " Belle Poule " hair-style and others. The 14th century had preceded him with the " gallows attire " consisting of a starched veil held in place well above the head by means of two long silver pins. " Thus ", writes a chronicler of the day, " we saw a Damsel, watching a tournament, being stared at as if she were some kind of wild animal, so pretty was she. " We could be reading a description of the races at Auteuil.

But not everybody was of this opinion and Peter des Gros wrote about these hair-styles as follows: " Heads which would have been bedecked with horns are now mitred and resemble stove-pipes. And the more the girls are young and handsome, the higher the stove-pipes they have. Through detestable vanity, they cut their dresses so low at the bosom that even their backs can be seen, and so tightly-fitting that scarcely can they breathe in them. And many a time do they suffer agonies to make their bodies seem tinier. As for shoes, they have them made so narrow that they can hardly bear to wear them and their feet are often deformed, sick and covered with corns. "

If truth be told, these charming young ladies were attempting, if not to attract attention, at least to show off their charms to best advantage. Up till then, the neck-openings of dresses had only been big enough to allow the head through while ears,

neck and shoulders were covered with gimps. The surcoat itself had been closed in front with a brooch called " gewgaw ". Now, suddenly, the surcoat was loosened and cut back in such a way as to reveal the tunic, belt, chemise and even —shocking beyond words ! — a few specimens of bare skin... small wonder that preachers stigmatized these openings as " windows of hell ", inspite of the fact that they were hemmed with silk, fur or braid. The cosmonaut style launched by Pierre Cardin in 1966 is reminiscent —if shorter— of this open surcoat.

During Charles V's reign, thanks to the good sense of his gentle wife, Jane of Bourbon, fashion eccentricities were only sporadic. But, soon afterwards, one sees the little horned " truffles " which surrounded women's faces grow enormously in size. What came over these ladies ? They transformed themselves first into rams, then into unicorns with those hennins " pointed like steeples whence hung long banner-like crêpes ! " This extraordinary hair-style entirely concealed the hair except for a love-lock on the forehead, generally made of velvet. Juvenal des Ursins wrote: " The ladies had horns so marvellously high and two large ears on either side so wide that they had to turn sideways in order to pass through the doors. "

Isabeau of Bavaria is often accused of having started this crazy fashion. But, in fact, the poor queen did have some excuse. Although too frequently described as the fine flower of luxury and refinement, she was —if truth be told— a big lump of a woman when she first arrived in France. It is not surprising, therefore, that she should have dreamed up a way of attracting attention by means of " high and long horns ", rather than a deformed silhouette. But she really showed how devilishly cunning she was when she decided to advise the ladies of her court to place little cushions over their stomachs so as to make their waists appear slimmer... Whereas, all she had to do was to squeeze in her own waist and let her natural padding overflow ! She also took

(Captions, left to right) :

Isabeau of Bavaria is seen here in her court regalia (1389). Sumptuous costumes, an atmosphere of festivity, sensuality, such were the inclinations of this queen.
(Bibliothèque Nationale.)

Headdresses, circa 1459. (Bibliothèque Nationale.)

Captions from left to right:

The Dauphin Charles of Orleans wears an upturned hat. (Louvre Museum.)

Louis of Anjou, King of Naples, Sicily, Jerusalem and Aragon, wears a hat with its horned crown wrapped around his head like a turban and a tassel or "paw" hanging down behind.

A group of women. (Bibliothèque Nationale.)

Refined elegance is pictured at the wedding of Boccacio, author of the *Decameron*.

baths of asses' milk and stayed hours in the sweating rooms, after which " cupping-glasses were applied to make her slim " (sic). So as to appear younger, both she and her ladies-in-waiting used ingredients composed of crocodiles' glands, boar's brains, wolve's blood mixed with all kinds of strange oils.

Little by little, the low-cut neck line increased in width. The bosom was raised and supported by a " corset " which was, in fact, no more than a short-sleeved corselet laced in front. A wire belt was worn high over the waist so as to act as a " support " for the bosom. Some ladies of fashion, insufficiently endowed by Nature, did not hesitate to slip, into the proper places, small apple-shaped cushions which they sewed to their chemises. A Strasburg edict dated 1370 however ordered that " no woman should support her bust, whether by arranging her chemise or by lacing her dress... " Just where. did the lawmakers stop !

Belts were of silk or of braided silver thread called " bisette ", woven into an open pattern which inspired the first lace.

On jumping out of bed in the morning, the coquette would begin by putting on a sleeved chemise of fine linen or silk, followed by the " doublet ", a kind of long house-coat made of cotton-cloth in summer and of white quilted wool-cloth in winter. This doublet was used for every purpose: as a dressing-gown and sometimes even as a bath-robe... doubtless for those famous " confinement baths " which women took during pregnancy.

In this respect, it is amusing to note that the young mother entertained from her bed after the delivery dressed as for a ball and bedecked in jewels, wearing her hair cockaded and " dressed in velvet ", in white or crimson satin or in cloths of gold or silver. She wore a choker around her neck, gold bracelets and was generally " more adorned than an idol or a playing-card queen " according to the commentary in the *Sinner's Speculum* in 1468.

Such receptions found the young mother's girl friends chattering at her bedside. These meetings were called " maternity gossips ". The display ended with the churching ceremony, the traditional Mass for women after childbirth. The young mother took part in her wedding costume which was a scarlet or vermilion dress —for at the close of the Middle Ages and long afterwards, young girls wore red at their weddings. Over the doublet was worn the surcoat, a kind of sleeveless coat, open to the waist beneath the arm-pits so as to enable the metal-work belt to be seen. The openings were trimmed with fur, braid or else precious buttons.

Following the example of their Oriental counterparts, women in the Middle Ages wore pumps, furlined shoes with pointed toes and bootees which were mainly used for walking around the house. When going out, these were protected with worked-leather pattens, or wooden shoes with very thick soles. In Spain and Germany, women wore very wide heels beneath. In winter, they wore boots and gloves made of chamois leather and even —horror of horrors !— dog-skin.

Smart men, while travelling, wore furry felt hats, pointed like beaks in front, or else a kind of big boater with a veil over it. Silver chains were worn as belts to which were attached the hat, keys and various knick-knacks, including those little round ball containers, pierced with holes and giving out scent. One of the most remarkable novelties of the last years of the 14th century was the " hooded cloak" derived from the Oriental caftan. This was the first proper coat, open and overlapping, with long sleeves, often tied with a belt and hooded.

All these fashions were exceedingly costly and lords and gentry who spent freely on their attire and food, were troubled by the taxes of the day. We sometimes complain about the heaviness of our own taxes... Let us take comfort in the thought that the problem is not a new one. As early as 1279, Philip the Bold and

Captions from left to right :

A provincial lady.

Forerunners of our tights, " Polish leathers " give shapeliness to the legs and wonderful slimness to the feet.

Fashion evolves in the House of Burgundy (see pages 52-53). By 1422, the bottom of the jacket had shortened into a mini-skirt. The beltless "dress" split right down the side. The hood consisted of a coif surrounded with padding. The horned crown was flounced into a cockscomb on top and hung down the side.
(Bibliothèque Nationale.)

fifteen years later, Philip the Fair, were already searching with their " treasurers " for ways to raise funds for the public exchequer. They expressed naive astonishment at the lack of enthusiasm on the part of tax payers to settle their debts to the State.

Both sovereigns attempted to force private individuals to practise economy by issuing sumptuary laws limiting the number of courses served at table and the quantity of clothes which they wore on their backs. The most titled lords were no longer allowed to order more than five " fur-lined costumes " each year, others only four, and a limited number of robes according to a decreasing scale of land income extending from 6000 to 2000 pounds. " Robe " was the term applied to all those parts of a costume which were cut out of a single length of material. Members of the gentry, owning a capital of 1000 pounds, were allowed one costume, and their wives two. They were not permitted to wear vair, squirrelback, gold, precious stones or gold or silver crowns; nor were they permitted luxury carriages or golden spurs. The price of cloth varied also according to the rank of the buyer: 30 sous the ell for nobles and 25 for gentry. In 1294, it was worse still: no one was allowed to own more than four costumes a year, nor clothes worth more than 25 sous an ell.

Fines of 20 to 40 pounds were also calculated proportionately to the social position of the tax evader. The most incredible aspect of this business was that a sixth part of this fine was given as a reward to the informer !

Just imagine what an uproar such laws would raise nowadays.

At the time, those directly concerned —or at least the young— took no notice. However, a number of " old crocks " refused to go modern and, following the example of King Philip VI of Valois, went

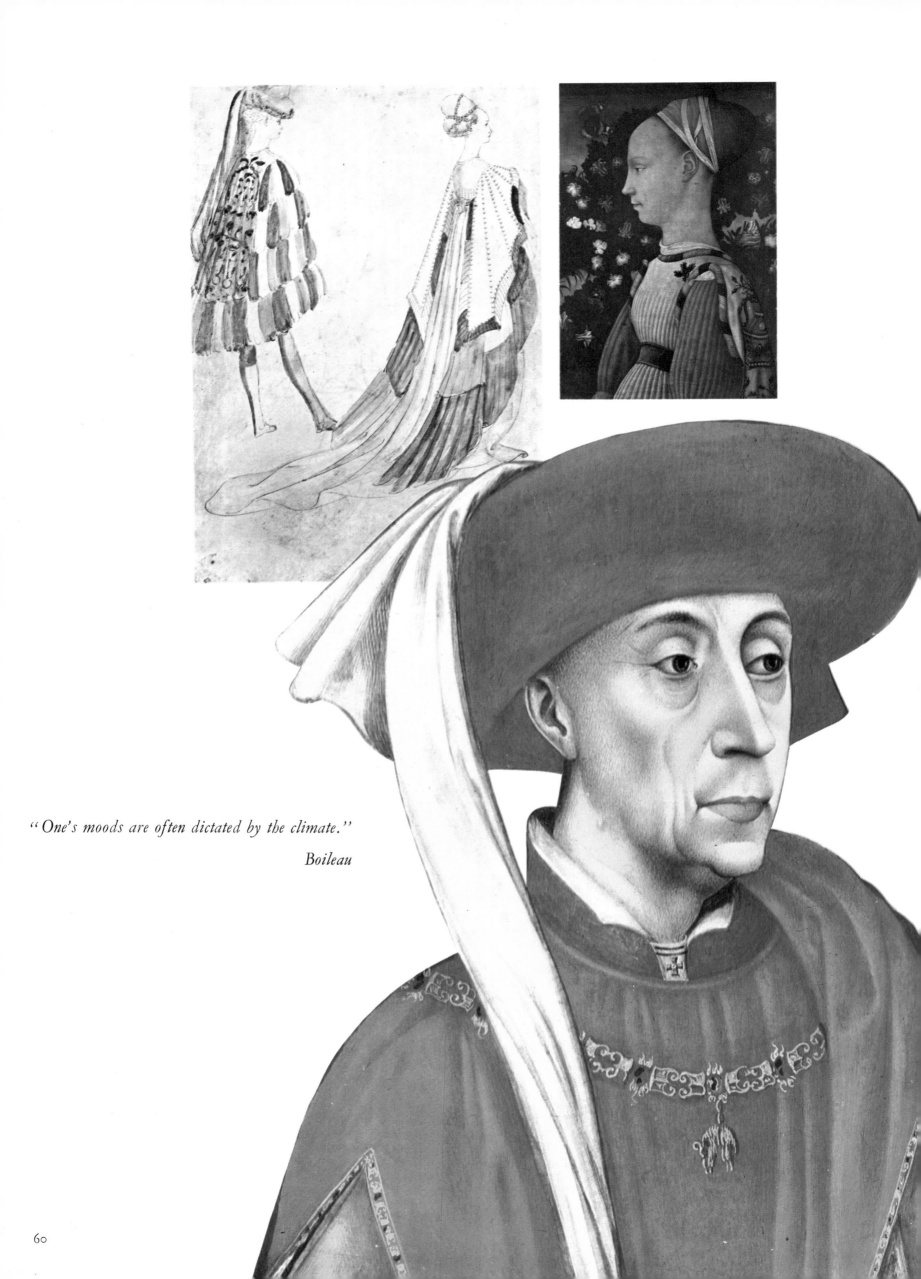

"One's moods are often dictated by the climate."

Boileau

on wearing the long costume with lacework hood. Senior officials did likewise, retaining the ample surcoats and the cloaks with wide organ-pipe pleats which represented, in the eyes of the people, the authority and guarantees of the privileged. People were thus divided into the " long-robed " and the " short-robed ". Furthermore, each profession had a right to particular colors which sometimes varied according to the provinces.

The hood also changed shape. Instead of passing over the head like a balaclava helmet, it was turned into a head-dress, trimmed with a roll and fitted with two tabs which were tied beneath the chin or hooked or buttoned to the shoulders of the costume. The hat itself became a ridiculous affair, pointed and almost devoid of brim, cylindrical and bowler-shaped with upturned or downturned edges... More ridiculous still were the unexpected trimmings worn with it: cockscombs of cloth, spinach-seed bouquets, silk garlands and fringes, feathers lying down or pointing upwards, rustling leaves and goodness knows

what other inventions ! Charles VII himself, as shown in his portrait, had some extraordinary ones made. Here is an example of such a decoration described in a ledger of 1458: "Two thick spools of gold thread from Florence, to form two buttons decorated with big tassels, to attach to a gold chain hanging from a gold belt, hinged so as to go around the hat covered in green silk-mock-velvet. "

And while on the subject of Charles VII, we can scarcely avoid mentioning his beautiful friend Agnes Sorel, one of the most elegant women of her day, criticised or praised in turn. True enough, one can reproach the beautiful Agnes for having " bared her shoulders and bosom right down to the middle of her breast ". She was nonetheless a leader as far as fashion was concerned. Did she not invent the hennin and the skirt fastened with a cord at the waist and wide behind, hemmed with a velvet band or else a strip of white fur ? A lady's rank was proportionate to the width of this hem and to the length of the train.

Elegant manners and modes marked court life in the 15th century.
(left to right) :

Pisanello, the Italian artist, designed these court costumes. (Condé Museum, Chantilly.)

Portrait of a princess of the Italian princely family of Este. (Louvre Museum.)

Philip the Good, Duke of Burgundy, wears the Order of the Golden Fleece which he founded in 1430. (Bibliothèque Nationale.)

In this illuminated manuscript, *Les Très Riches Heures du Duc de Berry*, Pol de Limbourg painted this portrait of Jean, the Duke of Berry, at dinner. (Chantilly Museum.)

Les Très Riches Heures du Duc de Berry is also a rich source of information on the costumes and habits of 15th century France.
(left to right) :

In this illuminated illustration entitled "May" young people on horseback wander through the countryside in the Duchy of Auvergne, one of the Duke of Berry's dominions.

"August" depicts peasants bringing in the harvest or bathing.

" A coat of velvet but a stomach of bran"   *(French proverb).*

In "April" young girls pick the first flowers in the meadows; fiancés exchange engagement rings in this illuminated painting. It is worth noting the heron plumes which decorate the young woman's hat... She has a small fortune on her head. The scene takes place in the château of Dourdan where the Duke of Berry kept some of his treasures. On the lake, two fishing boats drag a net. In the garden, the fruit trees, pruned and tied, are beginning to blossom. This miniature is from *Les Très Riches Heures du Duc de Berry*. (Chantilly Museum.)

65

GOLD AND PEARLS

"Only the king of a free people is a powerful king."

Gudin de la Brunellerie

The men who ruled Portugal's far-flung possessions wore the extravagant regalia typical of the mother country.
(left to right):

Don João de Castro was governor of the East Indies from 1545 to 1548. (Naval Museum, Lisbon.)

A Japanese wood-painting depicts a costume of the 18th century.

Don Vasco de Gama was an earlier governor of the East Indies. (Naval Museum, Lisbon.)

Portuguese came to Japan ladened with gifts for the Emperor of Japan. (Museum of Ancient Art, Lisbon.)

Alfonso of Albuquerque governed the East Indies between 1509 and 1515. (Naval Museum, Lisbon.)

"Style is not a dance, but a bearing."   Jean Cocteau

Styles of the late 16th century gave women a regal air.
(left to right):

This lady, depicted in 1586, wears the panniers, frills and furbelows of her day.

Elizabeth of Austria, married to France's Charles IX wore this gown while civil war raged in France.

Two harlots.

Anne, Duke of Joyeuse, Admiral of France, and his bride, Marguerite of Lorraine, sister of Queen Louise, lead the dancing after the wedding ceremony at the court of Henry III on September 24, 1581.
(Painting attributed to Hermann Van der Mast, Versailles.)

THE SEVENTH REVOLUTION

THE RENAISSANCE

The flowering of culture in the Renaissance also touched off a revolution in dress. Its roots, as we have seen, lay in the second half of the Middle Ages when a sense of refinement, the desire and art of pleasing — not to mention a craze for extravagance — had gradually preoccupied the nobility. By the 16th century commoners and even magistrates had but one idea; to show off their riches.

This · trend no doubt prevented the Greek-style draped clothing from coming back into favor, despite the fact that so many of the decorations during the reign of France's Francis I (1515-1547) were inspired by ancient Greece. Such simplicity and conformity did not go well with this urge to display a newfound prosperity.

The two people mainly responsible for this inflow of riches were Christopher Columbus and Vasco de Gama. By his discovery of San Salvador, Cuba and then Guadaloupe and Porto Rico in 1492 and 1495, followed by his exploration of the Central American coasts, Christopher Columbus was instrumental in promoting trade in precious metals. Vasco de Gama opened up the sea-route to India in 1498.

At the beginning of the 16th century, Europe was thus richer than she had ever been before and was to display a luxury never equalled before or since. It is generally thought that fashions were set by the privileged classes. This is true in a sense, but the part played by the manufacturers is of utmost importance. Whenever the clothing industry prospers, it can be seen to impose its new styles to the detriment of former ones. For example, in France, at the beginning of the 16th century lighter and softer materials such as serge and muslin allowed closer-fitting shapes to replace the old-fashioned cloth. Indeed, clothes were of unbelievable magnificence thanks not only to the quality of the materials, but also to the embroidery, gold braiding, pearls and precious stones with which they were covered.

At Tours, there were no less than 8,000 looms for silks (velvets, satins and taffetas) and at Lyons; manufacturers employed 12,000 workers for brocaded silks. The hosiery trade in particular greatly expanded: silk stockings were woven at Dourdan; velvets and satins at Nimes and Montpellier. Despite a snobbism current at that time which favored foreign clothes, a French law of 1450 taxed imported silks and another of 1572 taxed even more heavily linens, velvets and taffetas. Nevertheless dyes were perfected thanks to cochineal from Armenia, indigo from

" All in a human being should be beautiful, his looks clothes, soul and thoughts."
Chekhov

Baghdad, saffron from India and the Levant, madder and henna from Arabia.

Little by little, throughout Europe, Italian influence which had predominated until then, gave way to French fashions. However, as we have already pointed out, each country was subjected to many different influences. Thus, in the land of Cervantes, women wore coifs in the Portuguese style, skirts in the Flemish of French styles but in neutral or dark shades. Spanish women were so pious that, in the absence of their husbands, they would dedicate themselves to a saint and wear a kind of plain monk's robe, tied at the waist with a cord.

Spanish Coquettes Were the First Women in Europe to Wear Breeches.

Men were dressed in velvet from head to foot and displayed such studied elegance that towards the end of the 16th century courtesans (and even a number of middle-class women !) adopted breeches just like those which Yves Saint-Laurent designed in 1967.

In Italy, it was fashionable to wear the Spanish style costume with a dark-colored doublet, but made of silk and covered with embroidery. But Italian author-

(left to right):

The King's Swiss guards in the 16th century.

The "Jeu de Paume" player of the 16th century was the ancestor of our tennis player.

Lovers-circa, 16th century.

A masked lady in full regalia: 16th century.

Masked and demure, a lady accompanies her husband on horseback.
(Bibliothèque Nationale.)

ities under the influence of the church at the beginning of the 16th century banned indecent decolletés in Genoa, Milan and Rome. In 1514, Venice not only issued decrees limiting spending but exercised a severe control over the decency of the coquettes. Is this not just what happened a few years ago when shorts and two-piece bathing suits were forbidden on Italian beaches!

Francis I in France loved clothes, not only for himself, but also for his entourage. Believing that it was "ladies that adorn a court", he gathered the courtesans around him by inviting them to parties, hunts and games, creating rivalry between the most famous of them. Let us listen to Rabelais describing the male costume of that period: "Trunk-hose was either tight or baggy, long or short, always hacked or gashed with bows of gold cloth, satin or taffeta showing through. And always the cod-piece, rounded and jutting out, merrily secured with two handsome gold buckles held in place by two enamel hooks."

Doublets had shortened, but breeches bulged out. The slits in the sleeves, first intended to allow fine linen to show through, were now embellished with embroidery, piping, braiding... "slashes" were so popular that they gradually came right down to the shoes!

Despite his love of luxury, Francis I was appalled at the large sums of money which left the country in payment of precious silks. As a result, in 1518 he not only forbade imports of gold and silver cloths and other luxury materials, but forced merchants who still held stocks of them to get rid of them within six months.

In 1543, a further edict forbade men to wear cloths and trimmings of gold an silver. Women were spared these harsh measures; and they profited from this advantage right up till the reign of Henry II who had no such scruples! He even ordered that only princes and princesses of the blood should be allowed to wear crimson red. Their ladies-in-waiting were allowed to wear all other colors; but the attendants of the other princesses had to be content with black and tan.

It is surprising that, having now at their disposal much lighter material, smart women did not then return to a more supple feminine fashion. On the contrary, they now gave up altogether the hip-swinging walk so popular during the Middle Ages, and adopted what amounted to a straight jacket of thick starched linen: the "basquine", a funnel-shaped garment fitted tightly aroung the bust and strangled the waist. This "pike-shaped body" was supported in front by busk stays of box-wood, ivory, mother-

of-pearl, steel, brass or silver, which were chased, engraved and sometimes embossed. On a busk belonging to Anne of Austria appeared these words:

"I have this favor from my lady
of lying upon her bosom long,
whence I hear her lover sighing
who in my sted would long to be".

The famous physician, Ambroise Paré, told of wasp-waisted coquettes he had seen on dissecting tables whose "ribs overlapped each other".

The "farthingale" or "keep-thy-virtue" then appeared --- misnamed, for this new funnel of a garment, upside down this time, was invented in 1470 by the wife of King Henry V of Portugal who tried in this way to hide her illegitimate expectancy from her impotent husband ! A number of fashionable women had this starched petticoat covered with taffeta. Others simply used a triangle of rich material which was allowed to show in front, through the widely slit dress. The very wide sleeves of the chemise were gathered at the wrist with lacework frills and at the forearm with "muffs" of "slashes" through which gold and satin puffs bulged. But meanwhile, the sleeves of the dress were rolled back and trimmed with fur (a last reminder of the Middle Ages).

Prudish England was so shocked by this coquetry that parliament issued an edict as follows: "Any woman who, through the use of false hair, Spanish hair-pads, make-up, false hips, steel busks, panniers, high-heeled shoes or other device, leads a subject of Her Majesty into marriage, shall be punished with the penalties of witchery..."

In the middle of the 16th century, stockings were made of hand-knitted silk or worsted (wool fibre),

(left to right):

Philip II of Spain dressed in black, a fashion which he launched.

Portrait of a German painted in 1569. (Versailles Museum.)

A canoness carries over her left arm the insignia of her office: a long fur with tassels. (Bibliothèque Nationale.)

Portrait of Margreth Bromsem, by Hiert (1641). (Lubeck Museum.)

The knitting loom invented by William Lee in 1589 having been rejected by Elizabeth hee later set it up in France. It is not known whether the French word "tricot" (meaning knitting) originated from the sticks which preceded our knitting needles, or from the little town of Tricot, near Beauvais where stockings were made. Whichever the case may be, the art of knitting was already known in the 12th century when gloves and hats were knitted.

It was in the middle of the 16th century that the rigid fan first became a folding one. It was hung at the belt where it was used for a play of the hand, or for striking a pose. Belts served also to hold numerous other objects such as the portable mirror invented by Eleanor of Aquitaine, second wife of Francis I. Hanging in the same way, was a unique jewel, the "Paternoster", the same name which is now given to prayer rosaries. A metal-work chain which hung down to the bottom of the dress, it had a heavy ornament of precious stones or pearls attached to the end of it.

Men and women not only wore "chokers" — jeweled necklaces — but they hung around their necks enormous watches, real clocks whose weight gave them a crick in the neck. Our present-day youth are more discreet with their medallions.

Spanish grandees were the first to wear pendants on their ears — an idea which had come to them from

76

MARGRETA BRÖMSEN
NATA A: 1626. 30. NOVEMB:
NVPTA A: 1641. 20. NOVEMB:
MORTVA A: 1643. 16. APRIL:

Oriental pirates. Henry II was so taken with this that he even had his ear-lobes pierced as well as those of his courtiers! Henry III followed this fashion as did his favorite young companions...

The "Ruff" and a Taste for Black Become Fashionable in France.

The ruff first made a discreet appearance in 1540 in the shape of little frills at the edges of the collar of the doublet or on the sleeves at the wrists. It came just at the right moment to cheer up the black which Lucretia Borgia had made fashionable in Italy and which Catherine de Medicis had imported into France when she left Florence to marry Henry II. During this King's reign, a wind of austerity seems to have blown across France. The Lutherans wore only dark colors and Henry II wore practically nothing but black and white. "It is his livery", said Brantôme, "because of the beautiful widow whom he serves." This was Diane of Poitiers.

Ten years later, this frill slowly developed until it reached its full glory around the year 1557, becoming entirely independent of the chemise. Each country had its ruff. In Italy and Spain, it was decorated with lace from Flanders and was higher at the back than in front; in France it was evenly arranged in a single row of fluting which was wider than it was thick. At the close of the 16th century, there appeared a "jumbled ruff" made of several thicknesses of unstarched muslin (similar to the more discreet versions offered by some of our dress designers).

Under the Renaissance, the antimony so dear to beautiful Egyptian women reappeared to widen the eyes which fashion required to be "large and well-shaped as in the Orient." The "doe-eye" invented by Fernand Aubry is a direct descendant of this style of make-up.

Look! A Beauty-Patch

Beauty-patches also made a very remarkable appearance, a contemporary author tells us, in the shape of "pieces of gummed material, of silk, velvet, satin, black taffeta, cut in circles, rings, stars, half-moons... and even in the shape of a coach-and-four, such as the one worn by the Duchess of Newcastle on her forehead in one of her portraits!" Henry III's favorite young men preferred them in the shape of flowers, animals and figures. This king of an extreme and curious vanity wore at night a mask of flour and white of egg which he removed in the morning with chervil-water. He had his eyebrows plucked into "delicate arches over the eyes". His hair was cut into locks, curled and with a false bun in the nape of his neck, held in place with an ornamental comb. Agrippa d'Aubigné wrote a sonnet about him which ended thus:

"...with tapering chin
And face bloated white and red,
This was no King, but rather...
A made-up monkey, t'would be said."

However, it must be stated that in those days men used make-up, soothing ointments, perfumes and freshning lotions just like women.

Portraits by Dutch and Flemish painters reveal the differences between upper and lower classes in their luxury of dress. (left to right):

A crossbowman and his merry wife were depicted by the Master of Haarlem, about 1610. (National Gallery, Royal Palace, Prague.)

The Pawnbroker and His Wife was painted by Quentin Massys in 1514.

Catharina Both Van der Eelm was the wife of Paulus Van Beresteyn. (Louvre Museum.)

Dramatic simplicity was a characteristic of townspeople in the 16th century. (left to right)

German townsmen: the man at left is in mourning.

The French mourning costume for men hid even the face of the wearer. (Bibliothèque Nationale.)

A Scottish nun was veiled to her waist.

Flirting in Scotland was hampered by an outsized sword.

Spaniards wore hats like those seen today on Peruvian Indians. (Bibliothèque Nationale.)

"*All sorrow fears its own ending and thinks with terror of the day its own sufferings will cease.*"

Herve Bazin

One of the most striking features of Henry III's costume was the design of the top part of it. The cape had narrowed and shrunk revealing the chest garnished with... a hump ! This "paunch", which was narrowed at the bottom and stuffed with cotton, was an idea which the King is said to have brought back after a trip to Poland.

In 1580, the baggy hose became tight-fitting in the extreme, without a cod-piece and embellished with slashes at the waist. Stockings were of different colors, just as in the days of Charles VII, and soon the entire costume was gloriously striped. Certain costumes had up to eight or ten colors. The Duke of Alençon, brother of the King, was the only one to prefer plain green like the court jesters, and a number of people followed his example.

Throughout all Europe, disguises were the fashion of the day, and there were numerous fêtes in the "Turkish", "Mauritanian"- or "Wild" styles. Masquerades, processions, ceremonial visits and royal carnivals were each an excuse for fabulous costumes for which all levels of society gayly ruined themselves.

In 1579, Robert Estienne noted that "gentlemen dress in the Spanish, Teutonic, Flemish, Hungarian or Polish styles and the nobility sometimes wear an entire herd on their shoulders for a single ball."

And here comes Henry IV who said: "I want my people to have a fowl simmering in their pot every Sunday." And again, speaking to the clergy, he said: "My predecessors have given you words, but with my grey jacket I have given you clothes. I am all grey outside, but all of gold inside." He nevertheless let himself be influenced by the taste of his courtiers who wore clothes cut in flowered taffeta and had a personal embroiderer in the Rue de la Tixanderie. At first, these materials of oriental inspiration had been embroidered by Turks from Anatolia or the Islands. But very soon there appeared Parisian specialists whose success was such that their materials were sought after all over Europe. But by then the designers were running out of ideas and tearing their hair out. At this point, around 1590, a horticulturist named Jean Robin lit upon the idea of creating a garden of foreign flowers intended as a source of inspiration for these designers. This is how our Jardin des Plantes was born, later to

become crown property, hence its name "The garden of the King." In 1626, flower-patterned costumes having gone out of fashion, the garden continued to inspire elegant motifs for tapestries and was later used by students of botany.

At the beginning of the 17th century, toes became square and the heels so high — even higher for men than for women — that shoes were said to be "jacked up" or "drawbridged". They were decorated with a "rosette" made of ribbon. High boots in "Russian leather" came from the hunting field into the drawing-room, and even into the ball-room after Henry IV had congratulated an equerry for appearing before him in this dress at the Louvre... this took place in 1608. But two years earlier Englishmen — even members of the cloth — were already wearing boots at court.

Boots were tight and high — to such an extent that dandies had to soak their calves in cold water just to be able to get them on ! Over these, slippers were worn, held on with under-straps called "soulettes". Men who could not wear boots had to wear silk stockings, worsted ones being considered terribly vulgar. Noblemen used to wear three pairs, one on top of the other, to escape freezing to death. The story goes that Malherbe, the famous French poet, who was as absent-minded as he was sensitive to the cold, wore such a quantity of them that he always dreaded having more hose on one leg than on the other. To avoid a possible mistake he threw a coin into a dish every time he had drawn a pair on. Racan, another poet of his acquaintance, had suggested that he have them marked with the letters of the alphabet. The idea was a good one and a few days later, upon meeting him again, Malherbe told his friend with a laugh: "I am in the L's today"; he was therefore wearing twelve pairs of stockings !

The Renaissance period, so fertile in all kinds of refinements was terribly backward in matters of hygiene. Only "loose women" made an intimate toilette. The remainder were content to use variously scented little sponges which they slipped "between their thighs and beneath their arms to avoid smelling like shoulders of lamb."

No wonder that this should have led to a new taste for make-up and perfumes capable of both concealing the filth and covering up body odors... A number of noblemen, however, owned "bathing rooms" in which they held bathing parties as in Roman times. Nowadays our "swimming-pool parties" are more modest.

The court did not squander water... The Duchess of Valentinois once told Henry IV, in a fit of bad temper: "Sir, you stink like carrion!" and Queen Margot

(left to right):

This early 17th century woman, wears a "gasket" or fringe. (Louvre Museum.)

The beauty of Louise Julienne de Hassan, Archduchess of Austria was framed by a lacy ruff.

Anne Boleyn, Jeanne d'Albret, Eleanor of Austria wife of Charles IX; Antoinette of Orleans; Marguerite of France (Bibliothèque Nationale); Mary Tudor (National Portrait Gallery).

A Knight of the Holy Ghost. (Bibliothèque Nationale.)

"In paintings, a kind of mysterious bridge is created between the spirit of the subject and that of the observer."

Eugène Delacroix

Upstanding collars imprison the head.
(left to right) :

Francis of France, Duke of Alençon, Anjou and Brabant, wears a goffered ruff which goes right up the back of his neck.

Louise of Lorraine, wife of Henry III died in 1601, wearing this ceremonial dress with its standing collar.

Henry III, King of France and Poland wears a ceremonial costume covered by jewels and wears a hair-net topped by egret feathers and a goffered ruff.
(Bibliothèque Nationale.)

" A man should have the courage of his opinions."

Madame de Staël

Ruffs become collars and hose bulge like bloomers. (left to right):

Christian IV, a 17th-century king of Denmark wears a ruff turned down as a collar.

A gentleman in Lady de Guébriant's suite sports bulging hose in the "bourgeois" or "purse" fashion. A French courtier of 1577 makes an elegant if bulky figure in his gold-embroidered boots called "gamashes". White plumes intermingled with gold decorate his "bourdalou" hat. His cape is of cloth-of-gold.

A townswoman of the 16th century is as bulky as her neighbors. (Bibliothèque Nationale.)

displayed her "lovely hands unwashed for the past week." She had no time to wash but spent hours trying on wigs. Brantôme said of her: "I have seen her sometimes wearing her natural hair, although it was black. Yet she did not fancy herself thus and preferred nicely-shaped wigs." Marguerite of Valois had indeed a passion for blond hair with which she covered her own head. She would only allow fair-haired pages to serve her, whom she "had shorn one after the other so as to adorn her own head."

Wigs of Cloth and Tow Sprinkled with Rotten Oak Powder...

In the reign of Louis XIII, a few wigs were still worn, made not only of cloth, but also of tow. Instead of hanging down to the shoulders, hair was curled tightly, "thick and tiny", and gathered together at the nape of the neck. A fashionable quirk consisted of letting a single loose curl escape on the side of the head; it was called "moustache".

As today, half and quarter wigs were worn, mixed with one's real hair to give it a thicker appearance. Men of the cloth wore special wigs, sewn around a skull-cap. Sully kept to this shape until the end of his life. As collars grew higher, so wigs had to be shortened. They were then covered with little curls until "heads seemed covered with sheepskin". The fashion for this short curly hair was to reappear during the Directory (the Caracalla and the Titus hair-styles.) We have seen it coming back again last winter 1967-68.

These capillary arrangements were impregnated with a paste intended to fix the powder (of starch, well strained and pulverised) perfumed with violet for brunettes, iris for blonds and Cyprus-oil for others. This craze for powders was such that even nuns could be seen, walking about in Paris, curled and powdered !

Working class women, who could not afford these luxury items, fell back on rotten-oak powder which gave their hair a rusty tinge. A number of village women, a century ahead of their time, covered their heads with flour.

THE CAPE
AND
THE SWORD

" Wearing a long-flapped beaver hat, decorated with huge

plumes, and, as his insignia, a mantle bought from some

dealer outside

the Law Courts, bright eyed and smiling beneath his moustache,

which is twirled in a love-lock, he passes by, bowing graciously

to the guards who make way for him."

E. Magne

Cavaliers of the 17th century cut dashing figures with their plumed hats and flaring spurred boots engraving by Abraham Bosse. (Bibliothèque Nationale.)

(From left to right):

This young woman posing so regally is of the Portuguese nobility. (17th century, Museum of Ancient Art, Lisbon.)

This well-disguised figure is in reality the back of a lady kneeling in prayer. (Bibliothèque Nationale.)

The Heads of the Brotherhood of Crossbowmen of Saint Sebastian at Amsterdam. (Louvre Museum.)

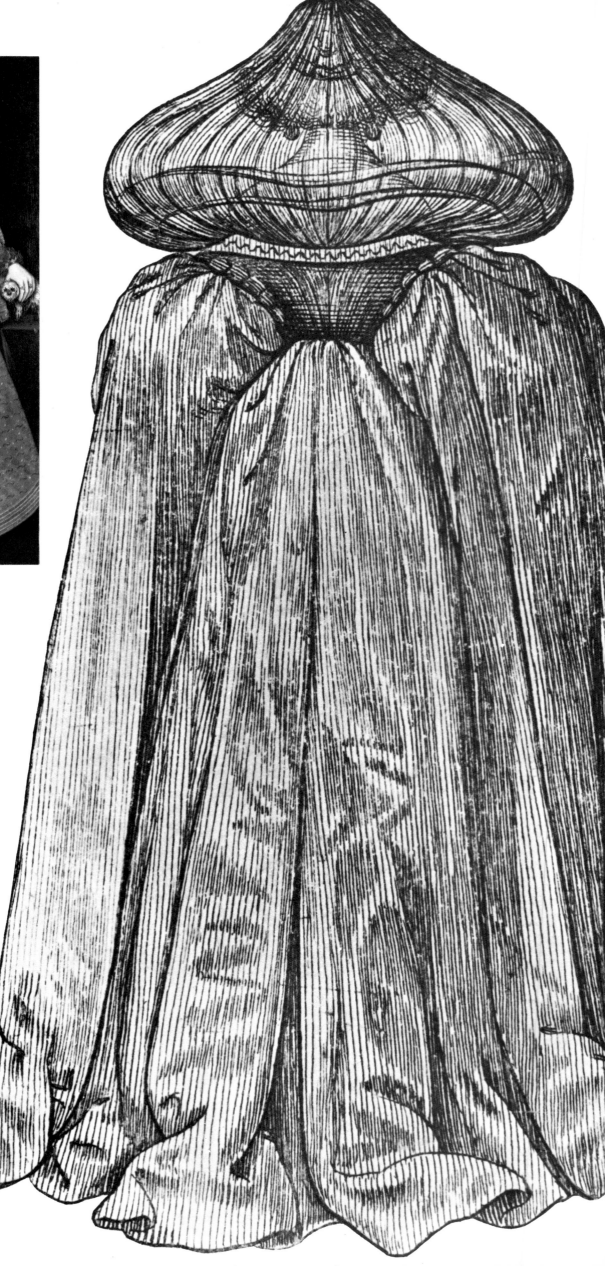

THE EIGHTH REVOLUTION

A HISTORY OF POCKETS

The reign of Louis XIII was a period of transition in the realm of elegance. One of the most important evolutions was undoubtedly the transformation in "hose". After being narrow and reaching to the thighs, they now widened out into breeches which were tied below the knee. Pockets were sewn into them until, under suspicion that they might hide a pistol or a dagger, they were placed over the cod-piece, then on the sleeves of the doublet before finally returning to the breeches, which was defi-nitely a more convenient place for them. In those days, these little inside bags were called "pouches" or "ladles". They were far from appealing to every-body. Many a gentleman continued to wear the moneybag or else used the crown of his hat as a convenient receptacle for handkerchiefs, gloves, money and papers (yes, even in those days !).

As for boots, these had become downright funnel-shaped while long garters made of taffeta, satin or velvet were knotted beneath the knee, revealing lacework frills. Trimmings were no longer rigid. Indeed all garments took on a more flowing supple look. The short cape became a longer coat often worn over one shoulder, or as a collarless mantlet, with short, hanging sleeves. Added to this was the satin "sash", worn over the doublet, folded and slung over the shoulder. Women found this so attractive that they too adopted it.

They also adopted less rigid farthingales: the skirt was heavily flared at the waist and trailed along the ground. To wear it correctly required swinging the the hips while walking, so as to tip the hoop of the skirt forwards or backwards and allow a glimpse of red silk stockings or the tip of the toe.

Sleeves in 1612 were still very wide and gathered in at the elbow with a ribbon and trimmed with lace cuffs. Shoes were "bridged", that is to say mounted on a high heel which made men and women walk on their toes for the first time.

Men's hats also followed the tendency to grow bigger. They were huge, and the grey felt "beaver" was decorated with an enormous ostrich feather which encircled it and floated behind like smoke from a ship's funnel.

One of the oddities of the period was the "green hat" imposed in some regions of France upon those guilty of business failure after they had declared bankruptcy.

Stockings and trimmings leaned more and more frequently to the reds... as did also the hunting outfit, which was entirely red !

Wigs were still to be seen, made not only of false hair, but also of cloth and even fibers. Instead of falling to the shoulders, the locks were curled into tight ringlets "short and thick" and gathered together at the nape of the neck. A fashionable quirk of the time consisted of letting a single loose curl escape on one side of the head: it was called the "mous-tache". Half and quarter wigs were worn as they still are today. Known as "corners", these were

fastened onto the real hair so as to obtain a thicker appearance. Men of the cloth wore special wigs sewn onto a small skull-cap. Henri IV's Minister of Finance, the Duc de Sully remained faithful to this shape until the end of his life.

Time passed and as collars grew higher, wigs had to be shortened. They became covered in tight little curls, to such an extent that they resembled sheepskin, which inspired the following doggerel verses in the "Discours de la Mode" of 1613:

"A lady's praise one never sings
If her wig is not curled in beautiful rings,
If her head is not perfumed and powdered
And spangled with bows by the hundred;
Four, five or six stories high,
With the tallest of buildings they vie."

The fashion for short curly hair was to reappear in Paris during the Directory (1795 to 1799) with the "Caracalla" and "Titus" hair styles.

These capillary arrangements were impregnated with a mucilage intended to fix the powder (made of strained and pulverised starch) which was scented with violet for brunettes, iris for blonds and cyprus-oil for the others. This craze for powder was such that even nuns were to be seen walking around curled and powdered in Paris!

The cavalier costume of the 17th century period included:
(left to right):

funnel boots into which one slipped a purse or papers;
foaming ostrich-plumes;
fur-trimmed coats and capes.
(Bibliothèque Nationale.)

94

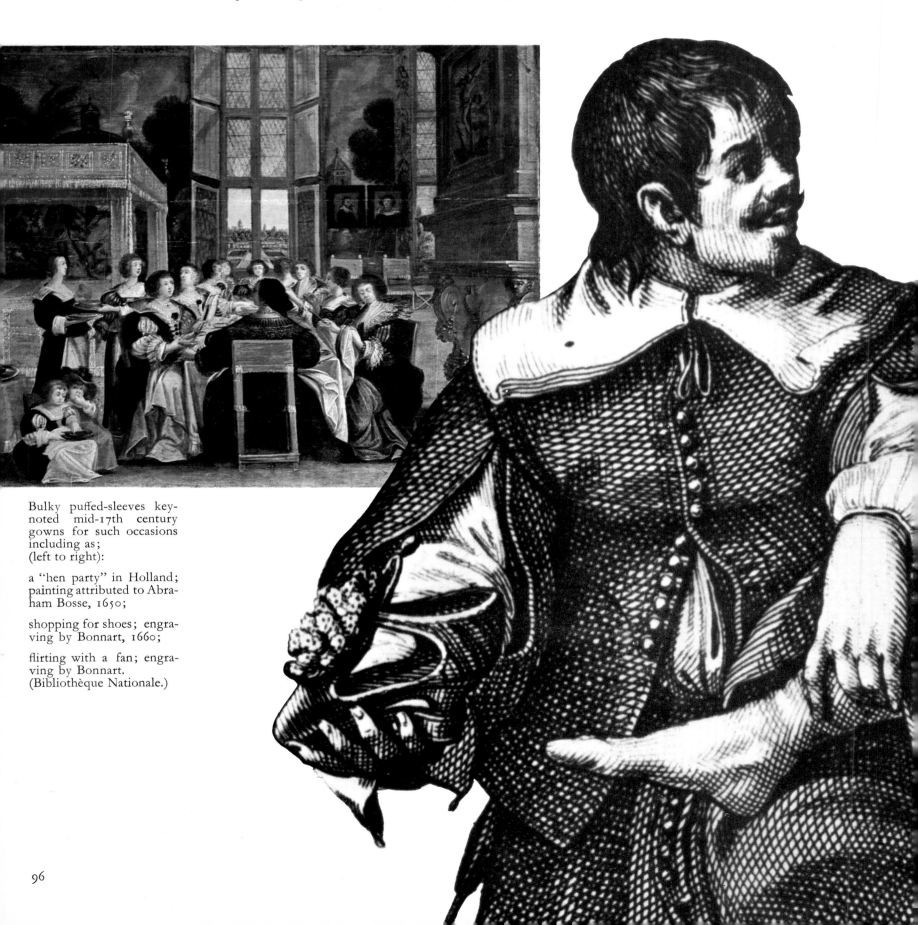

Bedizened and festooned sleeves set the fashion pace.

Bulky puffed-sleeves key-noted mid-17th century gowns for such occasions including as; (left to right):

a "hen party" in Holland; painting attributed to Abraham Bosse, 1650;

shopping for shoes; engraving by Bonnart, 1660;

flirting with a fan; engraving by Bonnart. (Bibliothèque Nationale.)

"Blessed is he who possesseth both

riches and reason."

Menander

Working-class women who could not afford these luxury items fell back on rotten-oak powder which gave their hair a rusty tinge. Some village women, a century ahead of their time, covered their heads with flour !

Hoods extended in a point over the forehead while the "tail" was pinned at the back of the head. This hairstyle was to disappear with the arrival of stiff collars. Only widows continued to wear this type of hairstyle thereafter.

In 1620, the farthingale became as "flat as a mill-stone" ! The fabric was no longer gathered material over the hips and skirts were hitched up by means of clasps. At the same time slashes disappeared from petticoats and dresses which were fashioned of flowered materials.

Between 1624 and 1635, clothes became greatly simplified. The neckline was freed. Ruffs were transformed into wide lace-work collars which spread over men's doublets, and sometimes became as big as shawls around women's shoulders. Lace-work cuffs from Flanders, Genoa or Venice were all the rage since trimmings had been forbidden by Richelieu in 1620. It is interesting to note, throughout Europe, the attraction of all foreign things. The more difficult it was to obtain a certain material, a type of lace or a feather, the greater was the desire to acquire it.

The dress became a kind of coat, slightly fitted at the back and sloping along the sleeves. The latter were slashed all along and were tied with a ribbon half-way down the arm. Even after this transformation, the petticoat-skirt retained its original purpose of a

close-fitting "jerkin" with long panels. Morning dressing gowns were called the same thing.

The "bodice" of the skirt, with a very low neckline, laced or hooked in front, was decorated with short slit panels. Necklaces were sometimes worn with them, wrapped around a bouquet of fresh flowers. Earrings became very important. Watches were worn at the belt and fans were carried in the hand. Rich jewellery was still worn in quantity.

Elderly women remained faithful to masks, but young women preferred small pieces of black crêpe, worn beneath the eyes "so as to be roguishly enticing and look whiter-skinned."

The XVIIIth century has always been known as the "Grand Age of France" — is this justified? Certainly so, if one considers the spirit prevailing at Versailles, the extraordinary prosperity of the arts, the

change in outlook, the importance given to foreign policy and the splendour of the *Roi Soleil* (Louis XIV). As concerns fashion, however, I am far from being in agreement. The stately magnificence of the Renaissance, the flashy yet elegant and refined styles of Henry III were succeeded, little by little, by a version in which a large number of clothes were worn one on top of the other and decorated with an incredible accumulation of furbelows, ribbons, lacework, feathers, etc. Never has the human body been so bundled up and bedecked as during the reign of Louis XIV — to such an extent that it was no longer possible to distinguish its natural shape.

And yet, the refinement of her way of life and her material prosperity gave France a leading role in the world. Our fashions spread further than ever. The magnificence of our embassies at foreign courts

The grace of dress and gesture typical of the 17th century are seen here: (left to right):

the king's page as engraved by Bonnart:

a merchant's daughter combs her hair;

Françoise d'Aubigny, Marchioness of Maintenon, was also headmistress of the young ladies of the Royal Abbey of Saint-Cyr. (Bibliothèque Nationale.)

and the fashion foibles displayed at princely weddings all contributed to impose French styles at every level. In vain did writers of the period lament that "shopkeepers are so well attired as to be unrecognisable"; in vain did the Paris City Council request "a rule regulating the usè of silk clothing and prohibiting the use of velvet and gold lace by persons of humble station"; in vain did the law forbid more than one footman for commoners and more than two (dressed in homespun and not dyed cloth) for gentlemen — all to no avail.

The self-respecting courtier tended more and more to change his clothes and trimmings every day. We were, in fact, the only ones in Europe to make such a display of our wealth.

In England, Elizabeth's luxuriant extravagance did not outlive her. The puritans took over and imposed their severity... in both customs and costume. The ruff was to spread down over the shoulders like a collar while the hat alone took on new breadth: the "spike-staff silhouette" shortened and the skirts shrank.

In the Netherlands, despite great prosperity, puritanism long forbade any changes in dress, which remained, rich but black and sombre, with ruffs and white tippets. It is amusing to note that children were dressed in the French fashion, in colored materials with ribbons, embroidered bonnets and shoes decorated with a "rosette".

In Spain, after Philip IV had forbidden the ruff, men adopted the "gorget", a kind of round stiff collar on which the head sat as if on a plate: it was neither attractive nor practical. On the other hand, fashionable ladies at last showed their décolleté. "They are thin and dark", wrote Madame de Motteville and, speaking of the Spanish "gardinfante" (a shape of skirt which replaced the farthingale) added: "It's a monstrous half-moon contraption; it looks as if several barrel-hoops have been sewn into their skirts. When they walk, this contraption hangs down and gives them a very ugly figure."

Men's clothes were to undergo a real revolution during the reign of the *Roi Soleil* in 1661. Called the "Rhingrave" style, it consisted of petticoat-breeches with voluminous folds, tied beneath the knees with flap-ended garters. Over this was worn a sleeveless doublet, called a "Molière brassière", which showed the chemise. Everything above the hose was topped by a long tail-coat, open and embellished with curly ribbons known as "goslings". And this fashion lasted for 25 years!

Madame de Montespan Launched the Pregnancy Dress
For women, in Louis' reign, fashion did not change very much. Madame de Montespan invented the

" As concerns their hairstyle, women are wrong to conform to the general fashion. Each should look into the mirror, examine her features, then adapt her hairstyle to suit her own looks and guide the hand of her hair-dresser. "   Carlo Goldoni.

(From left to right):

" Monsieur Champagne ", seen here brushing a client's heir, was the Alexandre of that period. "This scoundrel", said Tallemant des Réaux, "was sought after and caressed by all the women." (Bibliothèque Nationale.)

A lady, dressed for town, checks her intricate headgear. (Bibliothèque Nationale.)

A summer costume in Louis XIV's time. (Bibliothèque Nationale.)

"flapping" dress, beltless and floating around her body so as to conceal more easily the many children she bore to the king. Later, this shape was readopted as a dressing gown called "innocence". In 1672, wearing a negligé meant dressing all in black with a white apron called the "do-all". Little by little, as black became fashionable, widows adopted white.

Court ladies replaced the "body" of their dresses with a quilted corset called a "libertine". They ornamented the busk with "temple stones", thus called after a shopkeeper of the Temple quarter of Paris who fell upon the idea of coloring chips of crystal in the manner of precious stones which he sold at a cheap price. Strass was also very fashionable, invented by... a Strasburger! Then bows, ribbon-decorations and chenille became fashionable and were used in such quantities that one could no longer see the color of the material underneath. Beneath the coat, or "turned up skirt" as it was called at the time, bustles made of gummed linen were rustled loudly at every movement. These soon went out of fashion for it was thought that "overheating the hips might spoil the complexion." The skirt, visible beneath the coat, was covered with appliqué cut-outs of different colors.

Striped and moiré silks were painted in imitation of fabrics imported from India. Gauze and muslin, decorated in this way, were then applied over taffeta or plain satiny linen... In 1965, women wore printed muslins handled just like this.

With the improvement in raw materials, new and delicate shades made their appearance in France and were snatched up all over the world. It goes without saying that, in Paris, these were given suggestive

Whether hunting, hares or fun, Europe's ladies of nobility dressed with equal care.
(left to right):

Mary-Adelaide of Savoy, Duchess of Burgundy, as portrayed by Pierre Gaubert. (Versailles Museum.)

The wife of Mateveef, the Russian Ambassador in Berlin wears opulent jewels. (Charlottenburg Castle, West Berlin.)

A society girl wears a hunting dress, complete with a train. (Bibliothèque Nationale.)

Mademoiselle de Loube, maid of honor to the French Queen wears the same wig as her king, Louis XIV. (Bibliothèque Nationale.)

Marie-Thérèse of Austria and the Grand Dauphin, painted by Pierre Mignard, wear ceremonial brocades and jewels. (Prado Museum, Madrid.)

Madame Elizabeth Charlotte, Palatine of the Rhine, Duchess of Orleans, in hunting dress with gun... and fan. (Bibliothèque Nationale.)

" The life of a very pretty woman resembles that of a hare on the first day of the hunting season."

Paul Morand

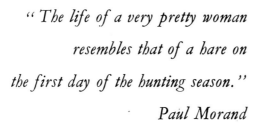

names such as constipation grey, rat grey, grey thought, rye-flower grey, sad love grey, summer grey, fawn-belly grey; she-monkey (grey-pink), young nun's belly, scrubbed face, migraine (red), sentimental green, gay green, dying Spaniard green and dead Spaniard green; dawn yellow, Judas yellow, oremus yellow, dying monkey yellow, merry widow yellow, lost time yellow, mortal sin yellow, love's desire yellow, kiss-me-darling yellow.

Some men and women wore muffs hanging from their necks. One of the pastimes of the day consisted of hiding a little dog inside these muffs. Mademoiselle Guérin, a shopkeeper in the Rue du Bac, even had a sign up reading: "muff dogs sold here". Hair was worn in "chignons" (twisted buns) or "passengers" (coiled wisps over the temples) or

hanging over the cheek "in the side-burn manner". The little curls on the forehead were called "love-locks"... not to mention all the other hair-styles such as the "shepherd", the "murderers", the "mice" etc.

A Fashionable Hairdresser Requested Kisses

Hairdressers took on more and more importance. Monsieur Champagne more or less created the profession of "lady's hairdresser".

"This scoundrel", said Tallemant des Réaux, "through his art in hairdressing and in pushing himself forward, was sought after and caressed by all the women. Their weakness for him was such that they put up with a hundred impertinences from him. Some he left with their hair only half done. To others he refused, after doing only one side of their hair, to finish the job if they did not kiss him..."

Complete with his musc-perfumed and tasseled kerchief, his

frangipane-scented gloves and his carved pipe inlaid with ivory

Our beau is all set to meet his lady at Cours-la-Reine

If this seems exaggerated, remember that women today also have a special weakness for the masters of the comb, who often have a more intimate knowledge of their private lives than their closest friend, not to mention their dearest lover. As to kisses, our hairdressers need no longer beg for them: they are smothered with them, as with presents !

In 1671, a lady hairdresser, Madame Martin, also had her hour of glory with a hair-style called the "harum-scarum". Even the influential lady of fashion, the Marquise de Sevigné, advised her daughter to adopt it.

History has retained, among other famous wig-makers, the name of Monsieur Binet, creator of the "full-bottomed wig". As purveyor to the King, he proudly proclaimed: "I'll shear all the heads in the kingdom to adorn that of my sovereign." Yet the Roi Soleil waited until the age of 35 before adopting waig. The first one made for him had holes through which locks of his own hair could be threaded.

Later, wigs grew until they became manes often weighing more than 2 ½ lbs ! Then, as they lengthened from shoulder to waistlength, the supply of hair started to run out and was replaced with horse-hair heavier still ! This monstrous mane was christened "in-folio".

The demand was such that the trade in women's hair, whether "dead or live", became established throughout the world and prices leapt so high that Colbert, Louis XIV's controller general of finance, decided to stop imports. But the wigmaker barbers, panic-striken at the thought of losing their profits, produced statistics and convinced the minister that the sale of French wigs abroad brought more money into the kingdom than went out to buy hair.

One of the most outstanding hair-styles during Louis' reign was the "Fontange" which, starting with a plain knot tying the hair on top of the head, later became an accumulation of gummed linen coils intended to support ribbons, feathers, precious-stones, etc. This fashion which was then called a "commode" lasted ten years ! Later, it as well as the objects which embellished it were given the most extraordinary names: "solitaire", "cabbage" "collar", "musketeer", "palisade", "mouse", etc.

As Saint-Simon wrote in his Memoirs: "It was a construction of brass wire, ribbons, hair and all kinds of trinkets, two feet high, putting womens' faces in the middle of their bodies. At the slightest movement, the contraption shook and threatened destruction."

This fashion lasted until the King, weary of these cumbersome headdresses, decided to forbid them and they were swept away as if by a gale.

REST HOMES AND BEAUTY PARLOURS DURING THE REIGN OF THE SUN KING

There is nothing new about American beauty parlours. The 17th century had its own and unique version. Alongside the inns, hostels and furnished hotels which were reserved for the gentry, sumptuous dwellings were built during the reign of Louis XIV to accommodate high nobles and court dignitaries on their way through the capital. These establishments were generally run by men who were experts in everything concerning dress and hair-dressing for both sexes. The greatest luxury and all the comforts of life were to be found there: "rest and relaxation as well as the best depilatory baths, mixed with perfumes and cosmetics which softened the skin and loosened the limbs." It was just like home; guests were served and cosseted and, should they wish to receive a lover, attentive servants would seem even to ignore the names of those they were serving. However these houses, which were large and well appointed, also enabled true invalids to find rest and peace.

Horses were as fancifully costumed as their riders for a tournament at Versailles during Louis XIV's reign.
(left to right):

A spirited stallion held by hostlers has trappings of fiery-colored satin with wide gold bands heavily encrusted with stones and gold and silver embroidery. The hostlers are costumed as Romans.

The Duke of Enghien as King of the Indies: trappings were of gold and black brocade, re-embroidered with silver and spangled with diamonds. The flaps of his jacket were garnished with large pearls.

The Duke of Guise is costumed as an American King. His costume was made of green brocade, re-embroidered with large emeralds, pearls and rubies, as were his breeches. His gold crested helmet was embellished with green and white plumes and the gold scimitar studded with precious stones.

An American Camp Marshall wore a cap of gold, shaped like a turban and loaded with pearls, a heron plume and colored tournament feathers. His costume was of gold lamé. His shoulders were tiger's heads from which hung fur pelts encrusted with dragons' eyes and precious stones. The bottoms of his sleeves and the flaps of his jacket were also decorated in this way and the trappings consisted of a panther-skin overlaid with gold leaf and studded with stones.
(Bibliothèque Nationale.)

> *" For the women at my court, hairstyle remains the most important thing : the subject is inexhaustible."*
>
> *Louis XIV*

Whether dressed for an outing or for staying at home, ladies of quality topped their dress with an ornate headdress.
(left to right):

Dressed for summer weather, this lady also carries a fan and a mask.

This striped boudoir wrap is made of Siamese fabric.

A winter dress is topped by a silky scarf knotted at the breast.

This summer dress has a multiple bustle.

A winter boudoir wrap has a long train.
(Bibliothèque Nationale.)

It was in one of these "hotels" that Louis XIV, in the days of his wild youth, met La Vienne who provided his clients, not only with pretty girls, but also with pills (a kind of pill of Hercules) which he concocted himself. For these services, he charged exorbitant fees. Later, the grateful Sun King appointed him to the coveted position of First Valet. In the "Laws of French Gallantry" we read: "It is a good thing to go occasionally to the baths in order to have a clean body, and one should take the trouble every day to wash one's hands with a cake of almond soap. One should also have one's face washed very often, sometimes the head too, and have one's bristle shaved daily." It is a known fact that Louis XIV only submitted to shaving every 48 hours, washed his face with wine spirit and used only cold cream. Neither England nor Spain had adopted the fashion for rouge and Addison, speaking of the Duchess of Manchester's arrival at Court, wrote: "When the proud ladies of France, who cover their pale cheeks with artificial rouge, saw this beautiful foreigner, shining like a goddess although wearing only what Nature had endowed her with, their look betrayed their confusion and a natural blush crept into their cheeks."

A number of women made themselves up with an odorous red ribbon known as a "red crepon" which they dipped into "an essence of Brazil wood and rock-alum, ground in a pint of red wine".

Louis XV's courtiers, as a reaction no doubt to the Roi Soleil's tastes — his favourite scent was that of horse-dung — were carried away by such a craze for scents that foreign women named the King of France's suite: the "Court of Perfumes". Following the example of the Romans, the nobility did not hesitate to spray their food with rose water, mallow, sweet marjoram and sage. As custom required that a different perfume be used everyday, the leading women of fashion possessed a veritable calendar of scents ! Jonquil, tuberose, violet, jasmin, allflower, rose, cherry, amber, frangipane, lavender and lemon were the main ingredients of the more fashionable concoctions.

The art of gracious living is portrayed in these paintings.
(left to right):

Princess Sophie of Prussia, daughter of Frederick I, the Sergeant King, poses with her husband, Frederick William, Margrave of Brandenburg.
(1734, A. Pesne, Charlottenburg Castle, West Berlin.)

L'Enseigne de Gersaint. Painting by Watteau. (Charlottenburg Castle West Berlin.)

Tea, English fashion, is had at the home of the Prince de Conti. (Michel Ollivier). (Louvre Museum.)

The Declaration of Love as painted by Jean-François Detroy. (Bibliothèque Nationale.)
A family at lunch was depicted by François Boucher. (Louvre Museum.)

In order to seduce her beloved, Madame de Pompadour was to spend almost a million for the sole purpose of replenishing her perfume cabinet.

During the Regency, dresses at last became simpler, there were less flounces and ornaments, less fringes. Skirts were no longer ballooned below the hips, the bodices was worn over a quilted corset but without whale-bones. "Flying" dresses came into fashion with a bodice which was tightly fitted over the bosom and loosely floating at the sides and in the back. "Pagoda" styles sleeves date of from that epoch; they were flat, open on the forearm and folded back. This was the Watteau style of which Fath reminded us with his evening coats.

In 1770, a book was published by a man called Bonnaud lambasting the use of the famous quilted bodice.

The title summarized all the reasons given by the faculty of medicine at the time for doing away with them: "Concerning the degradation of the human species through the use of whale-bone corsets. A work in which it is shown that it is against the laws of nature, depopulates the country and causes, so to speak, man's degeneration, to torture him at the very outset of his existence under the pretext of forming him."

At different times during the Regency, a long "apron" decorated with lace or braiding on the pockets made its appearance over the flounced skirt. Chambermaids wore the same with a bib atop.

THE FIRST HAIRDRESSING ACADEMY

The famous hairdresser, Le Gros, was the first to start a hairdressing school to which students of both sexes came in large numbers. The best ones were awarded medals. Class work was carried out on

(From left to right):

Young girl wearing a taffeta "polonaise".

An elaborate costume, in the French fashion, is topped by a "pouf" topped yet again by "Therese de gaze". (Bibliothèque Nationale.)

This young girl wears a taffeta "polonaise" and a gleaner's bonnet. (Bibliothèque Nationale.)

This costume consists of an Indian taffeta jacket, designed in the English fashion, and a double row bonnet.

Hairstyle known as "à la Victoire". (Bibliothèque Nationale.)

"Beautiful but no brains."   La Fontaine

"headlenders" whose beautiful hair was used both for the master's demonstrations and the experiments of his pupils. On public holidays when the weather was fine, Le Gros sent his mannequins out onto the boulevards to show off his latest creations to the public. Those girls who, during a period of four years, had shown unimpeachable conduct an docility, were rewarded. Le Gros made them learn a trade at his own expense.

AN ARISTOCRACY OF WEALTH VIED WITH THAT OF NOBLE BIRTH

Louis XV, known as the Beloved, had a taste for independence and sought to impart it to his people and his courtiers. Consequently, during his reign, we see commoners, financiers and businessmen setting up a life of luxury and pleasure for the first time outside the royal court.

Feminine fashion again became complicated. The double petticoat skirt came back into vogue, topped by flounce-covered panniers. The trailing end of the dress was attached atop this. When bending over, women revealed a considerable stretch of leg — but wearing trousers was considered indecent. Only ladies of easy virtue protected themselves this way.

Where did these famous panniers — which lasted nearly half a century come from ? Their ancestor was most certainly the bell-skirted Cretan woman. But one can also suppose — although there is nothing certain about this — that the farthingale,

(From left to right):

"The Comparison" depicts two beauties unabashedly comparing their breasts.

"The Confession." (Bibliothèque Nationale.)

Marie-Thérèse and François de Lorraine wearing nightcaps give Christmas gifts to their children. The little girl holding a doll is Marie-Antoinette. (Kunsthistorisches Museum, Vienna.)

"Doña Tadée Arias de Enriquez.". (Goya, Prado Museum.)

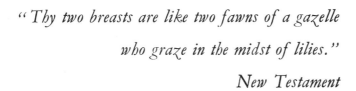

" Thy two breasts are like two fawns of a gazelle

who graze in the midst of lilies."

New Testament

having been adopted by one of the small central European courts, had reappeared in England during the reign of Queen Anne, or else that its appearance was simply due to the theater. Actresses of the period in both London and Paris willingly wore very wide dresses even when playing in Greek tragedies. Several English women decided to dress in the same style — an event which provoked considerable hilarity in the London press. But, funnily enough, these "hooped petticoats" left the Parisian aristocrat cold, although they adopted with enthusiasm the little flowered hats and the low coiffures of their sisters across the Channel.

Seven years later however, as a result of an incident which occurred in Paris, panniers were launched over there too. During the summer, two exceedingly portly ladies had hoops fitted into their skirts in order to air heir thighs. They then went to stroll in the Tuileries where they caused a sensation, and were practically smothered by the gaping crowds. The very next day, panniers were all the rage.

The first panniers were made of cane of whale-bone tied with ribbons or net. Later, they were mounted onto unbleached linen, thick taffeta, or brocaded silk. The earliest style, known as the "gueridon" or "funnel" subsequently took the shape of flattened domes at the back and in the front. These were "elbow" panniers for they came up so high that one could rest one's arms upon them. Theoretically, young girls were not allowed to wear panniers, but in fact, a number of cunning young things bribed their dressmakers behind their mothers' backs, to widen their false dresses and paid the supplement.

Panniers were for a long time the privilege of court

ladies until a certain Mademoiselle Margot invented a cheap way in which to puff out the petticoat. This was the first sign of ready-made. Market women and shop girls snatched them up. Sober-minded women were content with short under-skirts lined with horse-hair which stopped at the knees. These were known as "Jansenist panniers".

It was fashionable to wear white and soft colors. In summer time, bouquets of artificial flowers, ribbons or trimmings of chenille or frothy taffeta were attached to the top of bodices. In winter, bodices were hemmed with marten or grey squirrel. After 1770, neckerchiefs were fitted with a "cowl" which stuck right up from the shoulders — a reminder of the ruff — and was called "kingdom come". Hairstyles were still worn low, but raised over the forehead and were nicknamed "equivocal", "pamper" "in dispair", "mutton-head". They were ornamented with egret feathers, artificial stones, flowers, striped ribbons.

Hats and bonnets fell from favor. Only common women still wore cornets, the small coifs with or without flaps which was removed when going to bed. In summer, fashionable women covered their heads with a mantilla, and in winter, with a kind of hood, in the Manon-style. In 1964, our designers created the same sort of style for protection against the wind.

Stockings were made of white cotton with gold and silver stitchery. Shoes had round or pointed ends and high wide heels. Only courtiers were allowed to wear them red.

Between her laced bodice powdered wig
and plummed "poufs",

the elegant woman of the Louis XV period is not to be envied.

(left to right):

"Farewell." (Bibliothèque Nationale.)

An engraved and cut-out silhouette from the period of Louis XV. (Carnavalet Museum.)

An engraved and cut-out silhouette from the period of Louis XV. (Carnavalet Museum.)

Donning the many layers
of the fashionable costume
required time and aid.
(left to right):

Servants help their mistress
dress in this painting by
Pietro Longhi.

The lady playing the harp
wears the "hedgehog" hair-
style.

A wedding dress requires
an even more elaborate
hairstyle.
(Bibliothèque Nationale.)

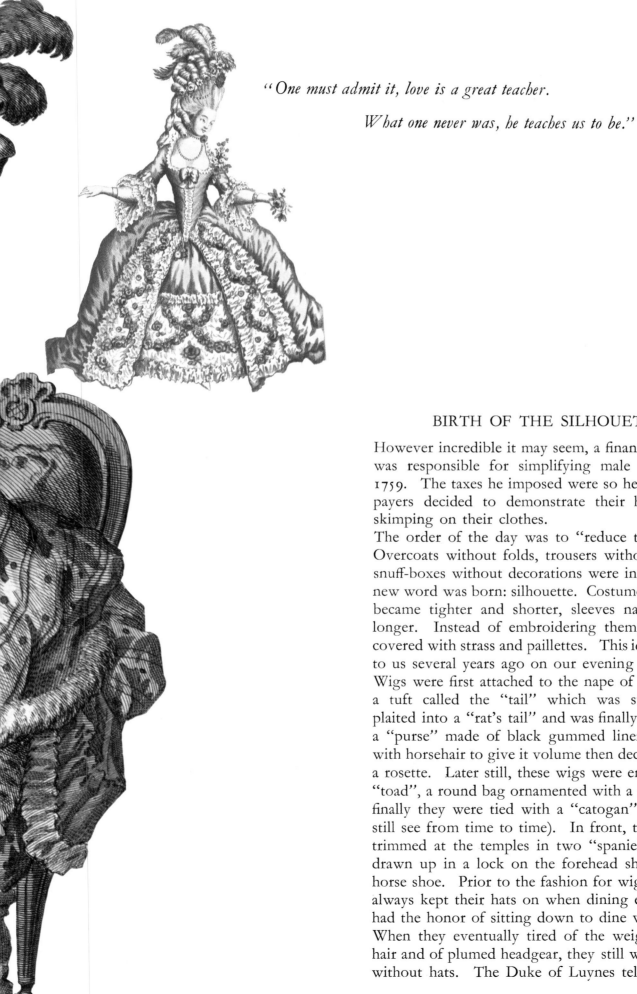

"One must admit it, love is a great teacher.

What one never was, he teaches us to be."   Molière

BIRTH OF THE SILHOUETTE

However incredible it may seem, a finance inspector was responsible for simplifying male fashions in 1759. The taxes he imposed were so heavy that tax payers decided to demonstrate their hardship by skimping on their clothes.

The order of the day was to "reduce the profile". Overcoats without folds, trousers without pockets, snuff-boxes without decorations were instituted. A new word was born: silhouette. Costumes gradually became tighter and shorter, sleeves narrower and longer. Instead of embroidering them, they were covered with strass and paillettes. This idea returned to us several years ago on our evening gowns.

Wigs were first attached to the nape of the neck in a tuft called the "tail" which was subsequently plaited into a "rat's tail" and was finally enclosed in a "purse" made of black gummed linen and filled with horsehair to give it volume then decorated with a rosette. Later still, these wigs were enclosed in a "toad", a round bag ornamented with a rosette, and finally they were tied with a "catogan" (which we still see from time to time). In front, the hair was trimmed at the temples in two "spaniel's ears" or drawn up in a lock on the forehead shaped like a horse shoe. Prior to the fashion for wigs, men had always kept their hats on when dining even if they had the honor of sitting down to dine with a king. When they eventually tired of the weight of false hair and of plumed headgear, they still went around without hats. The Duke of Luynes tells us in his

That night the court of Versailles fell asleep to a fine dream,

the alliance of the oldest European monarchy

and the youngest republic...

(From left to right):

As this lady strolling in the country demonstrates, not all French women dressed in as elaborate a way as the women in the court of Louis XV.

The "independence hair" style or "the triumph of liberty" celebrated the arrival in France of the celebrate Benjamin Franklin.

On March 20, 1778, the Court awaited Benjamin Franklin, sent by the young Republic of the United States of America to Louis XVI.

Memoirs that this fashion was widely current during the long reign of Louis XV. The male hat, at this time, had changed its shape to a tricorn, and was more often carried under the arm than worn atop the head.

At the same time, satin or black velvet beauty spots started to break out all over women's faces. No woman of any standing would dream of going out without taking along a box full of them. One was not enough. The coquettes would stick on seven or ten of them at a time, giving them various names according to the place chosen : "passionate" at the corner of the eye; "gay" in the middle of the cheek; "saucy", on the nose; "coquette" at the corner of the mouth; "kisser" over the upper lip; near the temple was the "majestic". If a beauty patch was large, it was a "toothache arms". "Playful" was over a dimple. "Hidden" over a spot... and "murderess" on the breast. Sometimes, these patches took the shape of a star or a crescent moon which caused an intolerant critic to write that "women's faces resemble the signs of the Zodiac."

Be careful everyone : the holy guillotine is there !

FROM THE REVOLUTION TO THE EMPIRE

(From left to right):

The ominous scaffold of the French Revolution cut off many a fashionable head.
In 1790, the French lady of quality wore a hat such as this.
(Bibliothèque Nationale.)

The "Jacobin knitters" in simple bonnets were considerable in number. They received 40 *sols* a day to go to the tribunes and applaud the Jacobins as they shouted their motions to the tribune. (Carnavalet Museum.)

THE NINTH REVOLUTION

AND THE FRENCH REVOLUTION

Striped fabrics were fashionable during the Revolution.
(left to right):

A satin dress in the English fashion had pink and green stripes.

A green satin jacket completes this costume.

Men dressed as elegantly as women in 1790.

The lady's striped hat matches her dress.

Gigantic muffs and voluminous hats were equally popular.

Cloth frockcoat with pink and black stripes is worn with striped gloves.
(Bibliothèque Nationale.)

It would be absurd to think that the guillotine when it started cutting off noble heads at the Place de Grève in Paris was also responsible for doing away with wigs and furbelows. French fashion was already less extravagant before 1789, but before simplicity became the order of the day, clothes reached an ultimate point of exaggeration.

Delightful, inconsequential, but also admirable, Marie-Antoinette was undoubtedly the main inspirer of these clothing revolutions.

Let us start in 1772 when she met Mademoiselle Rose Bertin, a dressmaker and one of the most curious figures of this extraordinary period. A true creative genius, the Queens' patronage gave her wings. She spent several hours every morning with Marie-Antoinette and did not hesitate to rent an apartment at Versailles ! This "minister for fashion" was also a pioneer; before dispatching her dresses to foreign courts, which were vying with each other for her creations, she displayed them and one could sometimes see as many as 250 dresses on show in her

Revolutionary young men dressed in light green.

The female version of a frockcoat has a long, pink Pekin tail.

Delicate colors such as These were popular with men.

This woman wears a perky, very Parisian "bibi" or hat.

Young woman wearing a pink satin "pierrot".

Strolling costumes striped from hat to toe.

A dress " à la polonaise ". (Bibliothèque Nationale.)

The faneyul harnessing invented by Daumont.

"Excess wealth is perhaps more difficult to bear than poverty."   Heine

rooms... It needed only mannequins to show them off! Her clients included the most fashionable women in England, America, Russia, Germany, Spain and Portugal.

By glancing at the accounts of this astute business-woman it is possible to have an idea of the clothing follies of the time.

Trimmings for a painted taffeta dress, puffs of French gauze, chicory brocade of cut crêpe, barriers and bows of cut taffeta, a frill for a petticoat totalled 64 pounds, or about $120 (£50) in modern currency. A yellow straw hat, lined with blue taffeta edged with blond lace, its crown of Alençon lace trimmed with bunches of pink carnations and reseda, a white feather a blue ribbon came to 84 pounds or about $165 (£68) today.

An English white straw hat, upturned and edged with ribbons; with a wide pink satin ribbon around it, flecked with black, a bunch of new feathers marbled in black, four white feathers and a bunch of egret plumes cost 120 pounds.

A fine heron's feather at over $1,000 (£400) in a box that cost $6 (£2-10-0) was also listed.

Mademoiselle Bertin Dressed the Chevalier d'Eon

Marie-Antoinette had such regard for Mademoiselle Bertin that she sent her the French political adventurer, Charles de Beaumont d'Eon, to disguise him as a woman before he left for Russia as a secret agent of Louis XV. This famous nobleman later wrote in his memoirs: "After Heaven, my King and his ministers, Mademoiselle Bertin was certainly the one who contributed most to my miraculous transformation..."

Mademoiselle Bertin was also noted for insolence and wit. One day when the Duke of Chartres — who

(left to right):

A lady of Rouen wore this simple costume at the celebration of the fall of the Bastille.

This pink satin dress was inspired by English styles.

This young man's green dresscoat is trimmed with braid.

English and Polish inspiration can be seen in skirt and blouse of this green satin dress.

This costume has a satin petticoat.

Pink taffeta breeches are topped by a vest embroidered with arabesques of various colors.
(Bibliothèque Nationale.)

"Oddness is dangerous in everything."   Fénelon

(From left to right):

Which of these French gards is the more ridiculous? Fashionable yolk linger at the entrance to the bath.

The long trains of ladys' dresses created problems in 1801.
(Bibliothèque Nationale.)

was courting her — was paying a visit to the Countess of Usson, the mistress of the house rose to greet him whereas Mademoiselle Bertin remained seated. When the shocked Countess reproached her for her rudeness, Rose Bertin replied: "If I so wished, Madam, I would be Duchess of Chartres this very evening !..". Rose nevertheless had a thorn in her side in the shape of Beaulard, a dressmaker, whose clientele was nearly as smart as her own. Madame de Matignon ordered all her bonnets from him and Monsieur Beaulard, who was no fool, suggested an agreement to her: for the sum of 24,000 pounds per year, he would supply her with a new headdress — a bonnet, an egret plume, a construction of bows, flowers, birds etc., or a wig — every day. He would recuperate it the next and put it on sale. Without being aware of it, Madame de Matignon became the first society model of the day.

Beaulard had a fertile imagination. He designed for the Queen an artificial rose whose petals opened and closed at will. His "granny bonnet" was a worthy forerunner of those sprung theatre hats invented by Albouy for Madame Steve Passeur. This Dr Jekyll and Mr Hyde bonnet, was intended to deceive any "dear girlfriends" or bigoted relatives who might be visiting a young lady wishing to appear virtuous. As the visitors departed the bonnet popped up into its full seductive splendour like a jack-in-the-box.

Hairdressers Ruled the Day

Fashionable women spent their days having their hair done. In 1770, there were already more than three thousand different ways of arranging hair, and this was not all! Monsieur Léonard invented the "sentimental pouf" where his customers sat. It supposedly enabled them to confide their problems, bare their souls and find a solution. One can imagine the deliberations...

"Léonard! I have the blues".

"Princess, shall we dress your hair with blue pansies?"

"Léonard, I seek a sweetheart".

"So be it, Countess, we shall strew your hair with cupids..."

In 1775, Marie-Antoinette decided that she could no longer wear young dresses (she was just 30) and she gave orders that the Princesses and other Court Ladies should no longer wear "pierrots, cloaks, chemises, polonaises, long-coats, Turkish and Circassian-style dresses" for ceremonial visits.

However, this was but a flash in the pan. It was to take another five years for the fashion for white to transform the Queen's clothes and the streets of Paris. Meanwhile the royal panniers became wider and wider

(left to right):
"Incroyables" tried to give the impression of being disgraced by nature and fate... The huge tie appears to conceal a goiter.

A fop in the Palais Royal quarter of Paris, wearing morning dresscoat, leather culotte and boots, top hat in the English fashion.

Palais Royal speculator in morning dress with a jockey's cap.
(Bibliothèque Nationale.)

(left to right):

An " Incroyable " depicted by a caricaturist. (Bibliothèque Nationale.)

A late 18th century family dressed for a sunday stroll in the country. Kuns (historisches Bibliothek. Photo Josse.)

These good people were appropriately called "The Invisibles." (Bibliothèque Nationale.)

Somewhat morbid is the feeling which forces an entire generation to remember

that it is afraid and to increase extravagances in order to prove to itself that the nightmare is over.

and were covered with bows, bouquets, garlands, flowers and jewelry. Heels soared higher still, to an extent that women had difficulty in walking and leant on a kind of crook decorated with ribbons. A little negro boy carried a parasol.

Needless to say, husbands and fathers were very critical of these constant changes in fashion which involved a heavy increase in their expenses. Both noblewomen and commoners wanted to wear the same toilette as the Queen. A number of rash young things accumulated debts. Families began to worry, couples quarrelled and fell out, the Queen was accused of ruining French women.

Extravagant Language and Hats

A new language as extravagant as the prices was created to designate each article of clothing. An article by a contemporary writer describing a costume worn by Mademoiselle Duthé at a showing of "Beauty and the Beast" at the Opera, tells us that "her dress of stifled sighs" was covered with "superfluous regrets", in the middle was a "spot of perfect candour", ornated with "indiscrete moans" and ribbons "of marked attention". The "Queen's hair" shoes were embroidered with diamonds, the "treacherous blows" and the "come-and-see" (buckles)

Simplicity and grace reappear.
(left to right):

A Frenchman.

This veiled hat adorned with flowers and the slim spencer with long sleeves were worn in 1797.

The casual twisted hairstyle goes well with this dress.

A daring décolleté, a shawl of black lace, and kerchief over the hair were typical of this period.

A dress with muslin puffed sleeves.

This garb is reminiscent of the "Incroyables".

Drapery and hairstyle remind one of ancient Greek fashion.
(Bibliothèque Nationale.)

(left to right):

The elegant line of the black blouse-dress is completed by a veiled hat.

" Monsieur Des Allures " in a morning dresscoat, on his way to visit his "petite amie", stops to talk with a man dressed in a surcoat.

Chopped-off hair was fashionable in 1798. Her Greek style dress is completed by an embroidered shawl and buskins.

Leather garters held up boots in 1798.

A horsewoman of 1796, in a lawn dress and linen Spencer, wears a jockey cap, the ancestor of the huntsman's cap.
(Bibliothèque Nationale.)

were made of emeralds; she was curled in the "long-lasting feelings" style and wore a "sure success" bonnet decorated with "fickle feathers" and ribbons of "woebegone eyes". Over her shoulders she had a shawl of "newcome beggars" color, a "Medici" mounted "in seemliness" with a muff of "momentary agitation..."

Hair-styles grew taller, rung by rung, as it were. Not only jewels and garlands, but also sarcophagi and square-riggers rose in tiers on scaffoldings ! There were the "frigate", "candour", "knight's cross" and "porcupine with upturned coach" hair-styles. Bonnets were in the "Punch and Judy", the "frivolous bather" and the "Voltaire" styles. Heads were also turned into gardens of fresh flowers. For this purpose, metal cornets filled with water were stuck into the hair so that the bouquets might survive the hottest evenings without wilting !

Colors were as wild as the headdresses: "puce" was all the rage. It varied ad infinitum: "old puce", "young puce", "puce's back", "puce's tummy", etc... For the color called the "Queen's hair", the dyers of Lyons received a lock of the sovereign's hair in order to copy exactly her ash-blond color. For shades such as "Paris mud", an approximation was considered good enough...

England Sets the Pace

In 1780, the craze for wearing white made its appearance in Europe probably blown in by a rascally trade wind from the "Islands", as the West Indies were then called. The ladies there wore white petticoat-like skirts with flounces in order to protect their lovely legs against dusty streets and dummy paths. Fashionable women from England were the first to be won by these vaporous skirts cut out of cambric or white calico.

Again the "English taste" was to prevail at Court with the launching of a "round" skirt, gathered at the back and supported by a tiny horsehair cushion placed beneath and irreventy called the "arse".

Later, a portrait painted by Madame Vigée-Lebrun of an English lady in a white cotton dress gave Marie-Antoinette a fancy for a "chemise-dress" called a "gaule".

England, with her mastery of the seas, was to go through a long period of commercial prosperity, due to her imports of cotton from India, silk and even linen which replaced wool. Perfidious Albion (as England was then called) launched upon Europe not only the chemise-dress, but also a masculine costume which gave women an amusing cavalier appearance, consisting of an overlapped riding coat with turned-down collar, cuffs and wide pointed lapels secured with big metal buttons. In 1790, these new Amazons adapted this costume to suit the taste of the day, that is to say in red, white and blue. And that is how the "constitutional" costume came about, white, with a blue coat and red "bavaroise", a muslin ruffle, close-fitting sleeves and a blue belt with long tassels. Two watches, ornamented with charms, hung down from two little pockets. These ladies even went so far as to use riding crops! The hat alone, with a high brim

Ah! these houses disapproved of by morality
and which the police
merely tolerate now by closing their eyes...

(left to right):

Frenchmen wore tight pants and chin-muffling scarfs.

A Parisian brothel is graphically depicted in this engraving.

Dressing for the day. (Bibliothèque Nationale.)

(left to right):

A grey velvet bonnet is worn with a muslin tucker "fichu", and a cashmere shawl.

The cavalier look required an open frockcoat, top hat and turned-over boots.

This cotton cambric dress is decorated with fluted flounces.

A filmy white silk dress is topped by a vicuña shawl and satin hat.

The slim lines of a ball gown are accentuated by a narrow stole.

A young man of the 1800.

A cotton cambric dress is worn under a tunic of heavy Naples cloth.

A merino-wool dress is topped by a tulle and flowered bonnet.
(All the above pictures come from the Bibliothèque Nationale in Paris.)

in front, still retained a few feathers and bows. It was the first time in history — since the Amazons, of course, that daughters of Eve were prepared to sacrifice their feminity to adopt a somewhat soldier-like appearance.

The end of 1790 saw a return to better sense, perhaps through an instinct of the forthcoming political changes. Bonnets resumed more normal sizes and helmet-shaped skull-caps reappeared. False locks were no longer used. Hip cushions and jacket tails were reduced to half size. Skirts hung straight and were mainly cut from toile de Jouy. Satin and taffeta were temporarily neglected.

The male dandy wore a round hat called a "bourdalou" which was banded with a silk cord and decorated with a red, white and blue cockade. His cloth frockcoat, tapering off into tails at the back, was wide open in front so as to reveal as much as possible of the waistcoat. The colored necktie was embellished with lacework at the ends and was tied in a big knot beneath the chin. Breeches, tightly fitting at the knee, were tied with rosettes over vertically striped stockings.

The Queen continued meanwhile to spend wildly. In 1785, Calonne, her finance minister, had to take 900,000 pounds out of the public exchequer in order to pay Mademoiselle Bertin, and this was only a part of what Marie-Antoinette owed to her dressmaker. When the Constituant Assembly announced that the almost empty State coffers had had to pay out twenty-five millions for the King's private list, the people rushed to the Bastille and seized it.

This was the moment at which the green cockade launched by Camille Desmoulins as a rallying sign, became red, white and blue.. Camille Desmoulins, lawyer and journalist had climbed on a chair in the Palais Royal gardens to hârangue the Parisians: "There remains only one thing for us to do: take up arms and choose ourselves a cockade as a rallying sign. Which do you want? The green, symbol of hope or the blue under which the American Revolution flourished?" The people tore the leaves off the trees and put them in their buttonholes. Later having noticed that the Count of Artois' livery was green, the Committee of Electors then proposed the red and blue of the Paris coat of arms, to which

" Freedom is doing all the laws allow."

Montesquieu

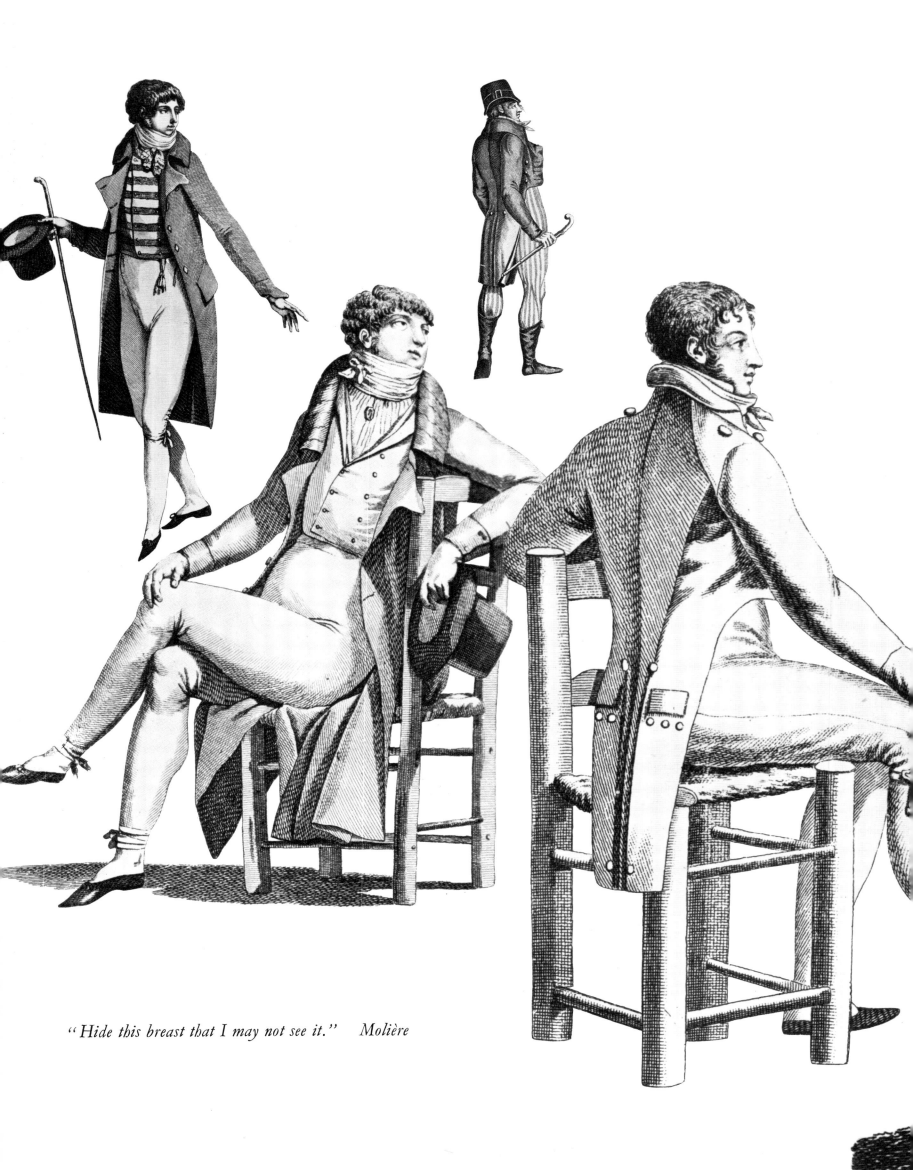

"*Hide this breast that I may not see it.*"   Molière

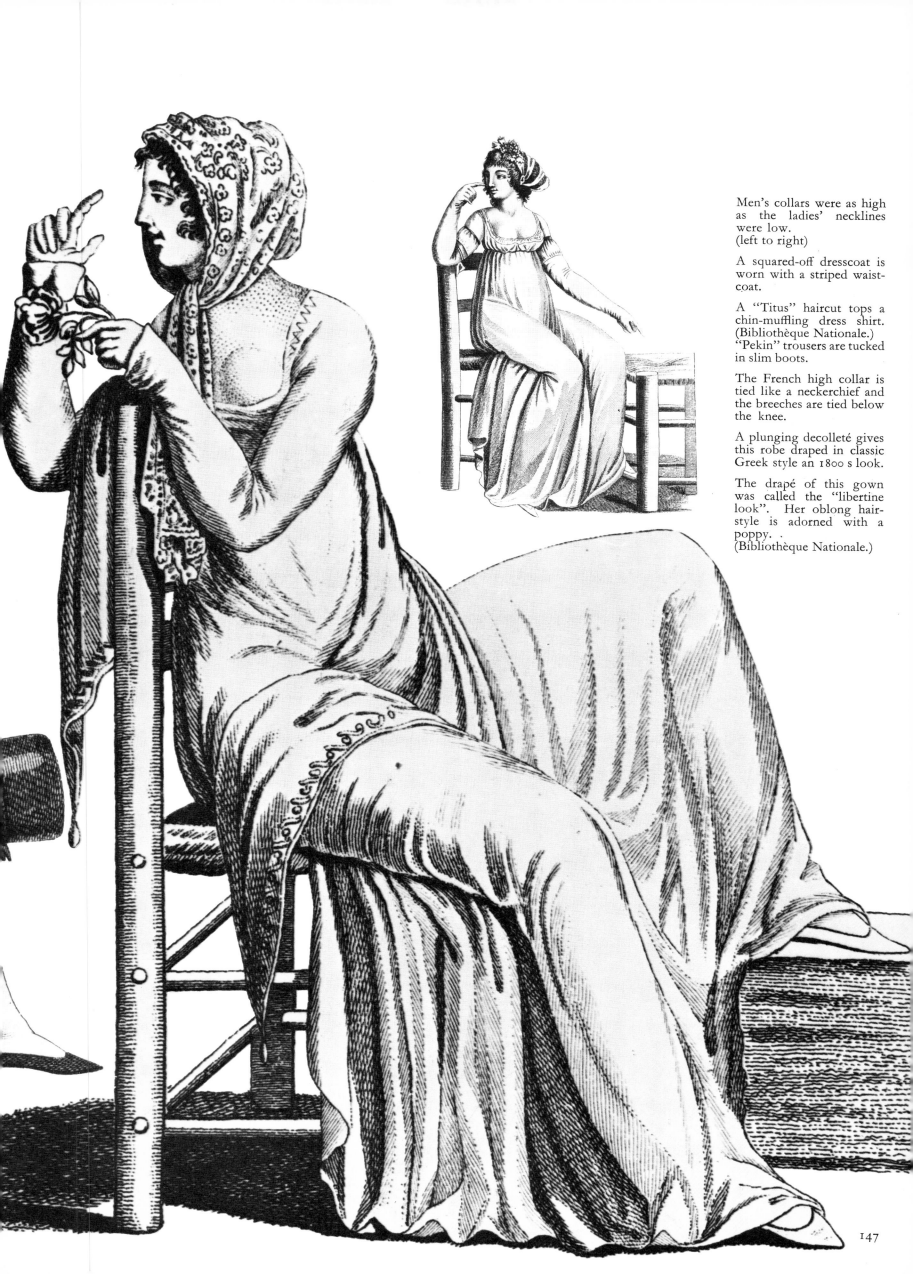

Men's collars were as high as the ladies' necklines were low.
(left to right)

A squared-off dresscoat is worn with a striped waistcoat.

A "Titus" haircut tops a chin-muffling dress shirt. (Bibliothèque Nationale.) "Pekin" trousers are tucked in slim boots.

The French high collar is tied like a neckerchief and the breeches are tied below the knee.

A plunging decolleté gives this robe draped in classic Greek style an 1800 s look.

The drapé of this gown was called the "libertine look". Her oblong hairstyle is adorned with a poppy. .
(Bibliothèque Nationale.)

147

general de La Fayette — newly returned from the United States — insisted that white be added as sign of reconciliation. As he enjoyed the protection and favor of the King and Queen, his suggestion was adopted.

Powder Became a Symbol of One's Beliefs

As wig powder was accused of depriving the people of their bread, the more advanced youth gave up using it. "Hoar-frost" powder was considered to represent a state of political indecision and partisans of the old régime whitened themselves more than ever...

The red bonnet made its appearance in 1789, in memory of the "Roman Republic" (the bundle of birch sticks surmounted by the bonnet signifying freedom from slavery) to symbolise the motto "The Nation, the Law and the King". Then, the Swiss mercenaries, condemned to the galleys by the King but freed by an amnesty law in 1792, returned to Paris wearing the red woollen convict's bonnet, of the same shape as the freedom bonnet. The democratic extremists were delighted and immediately followed their example.

The National Convention had never favored this bonnet. Marat wore a cap to the sessions and Robespierre, a freshly powdered wig and white necktie. The aristocrat whose acceptance of the Revolution was subject to reserve, dressed in black, but with a light-colored jacket, while the counter-revolutionist went into mourning from head to foot. Elegant women with royalist opinions wore white cravats, waist-coats dotted with little fleur-de-lys shields and the green costume with pink collar and a white ribbon cockade...

In 1791, loud-colored collars of cloth or silk, in pink, apple-green, sulphur-yellow or dawn-red were worn with dress-coats of blue, plum or grey. Young elegants, eager for attention, at balls, wore blue jackets, white vests and a bonnet of blue broadcloth, trimmed in red. They were called the "Muscadins" or Fops. Later they were called the "Incroyables" or the "Incredibles". They looked rather like our present-day hippies, but their linen was absolutely impeccable.

It would be a mistake to think that, in 1793, Paris was living in a state of mourning and fear. Cafés and restaurants were always full and twenty-three theatres

(left to right):

Grisettes make their morning toilette.

Booted, and swathed to the chin, this gentleman also sports an overcoat with five collars.

The well-informed lady reads the political gazettes in the morning.

A gallant gentleman, he has given his jacket to his companion as a sudden shower catches them unawares.
(Bibliothèque Nationale.)

did good business! Nevertheless the promissory notes issued by the French Revolutionary government continued to depreciate and most people were forced to use the clothes which they had worn before and during the Revolution. According to Quicherat, Bonaparte was extremely glad to obtain a length of cloth from Madame Tallien's valet, with which to make himself a costume. Simplicity was now the order of the day. Women adopted the striped muslin dress, gathered in at the waist with a wide belt. Curls and scaffolded hair-styles disappeared, to be replaced by huge piped bonnets, decorated with big cockades. However, bosoms were still very much in evidence and necklines were plunging. They were concealed by a light shawl, crossed over in front and tied behind. The fullness thus obtained compensated for any deficiencies on the part of Mother Nature... Men also chose freedom, forsaking ruffles, cuffs, purses and swords, thus accomplishing the ninth revolution in fashion.

This revolution affected not only clothes, but industry and commerce. For several years the weavers of Lyons, the workers of Valenciennes and Saint-Quentin were to be unemployed owing to the loss of their rich clientele. No longer were silks, cambrics and buckrams exported...

In the face of this crisis, Marat admitted: "I should not be surprised if, in twenty years from now, not a single worker can be found in Paris capable of making a hat or a pair of shoes."

During the Directory, the "Incredibles" went about with enormous spectacles over their noses and with two-pointed cocked hats in their hands. They wore locks of hair flattened over their temples like "dog's ears" and raised behind in a bun, held in place with a curved comb. In the street, they covered this "guillotine" hair-style with a two-cornered hat which was often outsize and the aftermost point of which scratched their backs. In place of ruffles, they wore "scrofulous" neckties which hid their chin up to the lower lip. Breeches were made to bag out and were buttoned over the knees so as to give a knock-kneed look to the legs. Shoes were pointed. If we add to all this a knobbly stick we have a fair idea of what these people looked like.

But, a little while later, young people became bored with long hair and had it cut in the "Brutus" fashion (with a kind of fringe in front and shaved at the back of the neck) to be followed by the "Titus" style, shorter still; finally, the hair was allowed to grow again and heads were covered with curls in the "Caracalla" style.

The fair sex did not wish to be outdone in originality. The "Merveilleuses" wore tunics in the "Ceres" and "Minerva" styles, dresses in the "Diana" and "Omphale" styles with short trains hanging over the right arm. Sandals were in the "Greek" style and hoods in the "Pamela" style tied beneath the chin with ribbons and a huge brim sticking out in front like a visor. Wishing to imitate the men, these ladies shaved the napes of their necks and wore their hair short and curly. The height of elegance consisted in studding their hair with diamonds: this was known as having one's hair "sprinkled"... (with drops of water).

It was considered good taste to display a certain paleness and to make excessive use of sweet perfumes. Both "Merveilleuses" and "Incroyables" left a scented trail behind them.

One evening in the salon at the Luxembourg Palace,

Bonaparte, then First Consul,

on seeing Josephine's friends exhibiting their provocative neckline,

said in a crisis of modesty,

"You can well see that these ladies are nude!"

It was accepted as such and dresses soon changed.

151

Ancestors of the Jerk, "La Sauteuse"

Beautiful Madame Tallien Started an Antique Style and Threw Propriety (and her Chemise) to the Winds.

Thérésa Cabarus — who, along with her lover Tallien, had narrowly escaped being guillotined by Robespierre — displayed a reckless luxury as soon as the tyrant was dead. Tallien then married her. She was not yet 21, had the body of a goddess and an unbridled taste for luxury. She appeared at the Opera ball with gold rings on her toes and did not hesitate to show herself with her bare breasts held in a diamond net. Her influence changed the fashion in colors: "gazelle" white was foresaken in favor of shades such as "pale and startled canary" yellow and "fly's backside" violet !

Madame Tallien, not content with throwing anathema upon starch (these ladies all but wetted their clothing in an effort to show off their contours), gave up petticoats and carried indecency to the point of doing away with the chemise ! "Women have been wearing them for more than two thousand years", she said, "they are so tiresomely old-fashioned !"
Wigs were worn in the "fiddle-de-dee", "passionate

heart", "young-lover-gone" and "risky roll-me-over" styles. An upturned hair-styles even made its appearance. It was called "the victim" in memory of the guillotine.
Up-to-date women never wore the same shade of hair two days running and Madame Tallien, who had revived the fashion for colored wigs, owned no less than thirty of them in graded shades so as not to be caught unaware by a change of tons.
Just like Marie-Antoinette, Thérésa had her fashion ministers: Nancy whom she considered the only dressmaker capable of cutting necklines in the Greek style, Madame Raimbaut who specialized in Roman drapes, and Coppe who fitted her tiny feet with ribboned buskins tied in the middle of the leg with a tassel.
The handkerchief was no longer hidden in the "devil's stoop" (pit of the stomach) but in a "reticule" (name given to the Roman game-bag) which was soon to be called "ridicule". It was a kind of alms-purse. And the "Women's Fashion Journal" wrote: "It is possible to leave one's husband, never one's handbag."
And now came the Empire style which, despite the

and "La Poule" also enabled the dancers to get rid of their inhibitions.

(left to right):

Two ebulliant gentlemen aid a trembling third to skate.

"La Sauteuse" and "la Poule" were all the rage in 1827 in Paris.
(Bibliothèque Nationale.)

To be up to date, one must talk about horses, ride them and have an English accent.

Parisian mannerisms of the 1800s.
(left to right):

The famous meringues of Paris' Le Perron.

"La Bouillotte", engraved by Bozio in 1800 was the first of five "Parisian dress" scenes published in Paris by the "Bureau du Journal des Dames". This picture recalls the atmosphere of the gambling salons frequented by Talleyrand, whose reputation as a gambler was strongly established while still young and remained throughout his life.

Anglomania.

Stroll on horseback.
(Bibliothèque Nationale.)

richness of the silks used and its high waistline, completed the cycle which had started before the fall of the Bastille. It was the final outcome of the antique-style, clinging and transparent, which had been favored by women during the Consulate. For the real revolution came about in 1788 when the taste for English and West Indian styles did away with panniers and frills and flooded Europe with white cotton dresses, decorated with plain shawls that they tied below the breasts.

Napoleon, striving to make his court the most brilliant in Europe, set about to revive luxury once more. He distributed money liberally (there was no lack of it; victories are so profitable... just so long as the occupation lasts !). The wives of the marshals vied with each other in elegance.

The First Great Dress Designer : Leroy

The fashionable dress designer of the day was called Leroy. He had been a hairdresser before the Revolution, but the guillotine had spoilt his taste for heads

"*Si tu ne m'aimes pas, je t'aime*
Et si je t'aime, prends garde à toi..."
(Carmen)

(left to right):

Chatting, flirting and strolling during Emperor Napoleon's reign. (Bibliothèque Nationale.)

and he had gone into fashion... which had enabled him the more easily to play turncoat. He easily changed over from the aristocracy to "wenches who blow their noses with their fingers" as an amusing chronicler of those days put it. But it must be said that these wenches were chic and knew how to wear the most daring fashions gracefully. Leroy beautifully reproduced the Greek tunic which was then fashionable and gave it a little Parisian touch which was indispensable. He was a precursor of Dior who loved sumptuousness and unusual colors. His first stroke of genius was to take on as his partner a certain Madame Bonneau, who not only brought him her money but also her personal good taste. She displayed Leroy's creations with such elegance that all the women rushed to the Rue de la Loi to be dressed by him.

Once he had made his name, Leroy wanted to extend his business. For this purpose he did not hesitate to take on a second partner — a dressmaker this time — who set him up in the Rue Richelieu in very stylish

quarters. Madame Raimbaut was already famous and had earned for herself the nick-name of "Michelangelo of fashion". The association soon prospered. Leroy met Josephine during the Directory and, after her marriage, she ordered all her dresses from him. He became dress-designer to the court and had every hope of being allowed to handle the coronation on his own. But Napoleon who had jokingly said to him in one of his good-tempered moments: "A man like you needed a man like me", preferred to entrust the sketches of the costumes to the painter Isabey, and the settings to the painter David. Nevertheless, Leroy's execution of the models was a brilliant success for him. All the European princesses wished to be dressed by him. Yet his prices were somewhat staggering, translated in terms of present-day francs: a ceremonial court robe cost 1500 Francs or $ 300 (£ 127) in current money and ordinary dresses cost 150 to 600 Francs. Lightweight materials gave way to thick silks and richly embroidered velvets and satins. One could buy at Leroy's — just as we can nowadays

" *Au café des mille colonnes,*
Sans peine on reconnaît Vénus,
   Dieu des plaisirs tu la couronnes
Avec les fleurs du Dieu Plautus."

The Palais Royal singer.

(left to right):
The young Napoleon II, titular king of Rome, as charmingly portrayed by Sales. (Schönbrunn Castle, Vienna Museum.)
Portrait of Queen Louise, first wife of William II, painted by Grassi. (Charlottenburg Castle West Berlin.)
Ingres captured the calm beauty of "Mme et Mlle Rivière". (Louvre Museum.)

at our famous dressmakers — not only coats and dresses but embroidered and openwork stockings, perfumed gloves, spangled or hand-painted fans, many-colored shawls, flimsy scarves and crazy hats... This is how Auger, a chronicler of the time, describes this Leroy: "He had beautiful hands with pink fingernails. He often received his inferiors in his dressing room and is said to have taken perfumed baths".

If we refer to the Fashion Almanach of 1814, we read: "When men start to take an interest in feminine things, this identity of taste could lead one to think that nature might well have made some mistake in their case..." Even in those days, there was nothing new under the sun.

Unlike our present-day designers, Leroy never repeated the same dress twice and elegant women had no reason to fear a meeting with women-friends (or enemies) dressed like themselves! Lucky women! Even at the height of disaster, fashionable women of the Empire continued to order dresses for themselves. During Napoleon's retreat from Russia, Queen Hortense (Josephine's daughter) asked Leroy to make her up a fancy dress worth 14 000 Francs (nearly $ 2,800 or £ 1 200). Pauline Bonaparte, the Emperor's favorite sister, was renewing her entire wardrobe at great expense even as Napoleon was sailing for Saint-Helena and exile.

As for Josephine, during the same period and also at Leroy's, she ran up a bill of 150 000 Francs which were in fact never paid.

Curiously enough, Juliette Récamier who played a leading role in high society, never dressed at Leroy's She remained faithful to white muslin dresses right up to her death.

NARROW WAISTS AND TOP HATS

" The small posters are full of attractive girls from 18
to 22 years of age,
of the best-natured character,
of the most attractive appearance,
who know, happily, a little of everything..."
Aulard

(left to right):

The frockcoat is cut English fashion and the trousers shaped in the Russian manner.

Watching the races at Longchamps required a suitable costume. (Bibliothèque Nationale.)

Both ladies and gentlemen in 1820 dressed with equal dash. (Carnavalet Museum.)

(From left to right):

Dressed to attend a ball, the gentleman wears a cloth coat adorned with velvet, tresses and gold tassels. (Bibliothèque Nationale, Paris.)

A handsome couple of the early 1800s: Madame Seriziat with her child (left) and Monsieur in riding costume (right). (Louvre Museum.)

Trousers were bell-bottomed in the London of 1830. (Bibliothèque Nationale.)

Dressed to the nines, this gentleman wears a balloon hat, piqué shawl-vest and foot-cut trousers (1820).

The frockcoat is lined with white levantine and the lady's blond-lace silk dress has an embroidered taffeta bodice.

A top hat in the American style and boots in the Russian style (1819). (Bibliothèque Nationale.)

I can only be foppish when dressed in an irreprochable manner.

Merely lose a button and my evening is poisoned.   Stendhal

THE TENTH REVOLUTION

BRITISH MEN OF FASHION

It was in 1824 that the return of the corset launched this revolution. The waist was back in its proper place and round skirts were lightly gathered over the hips. This feminine and charming fashion recalled gowns worn by the pretty ladies of Cnossus, Crete, in 1500 B.C.

It is interesting to note that from the 19th century onwards, male and female costume would no longer undergo the profound changes of the Middle Ages or Antiquity. Only details would vary and at an increasingly rapid rate as we approach our own times.

As François Boucher so rightly says in *History of Clothing :* "Henceforth it becomes difficult to follow the many variations in fashion. The evolution in costume can no longer be described in any but general terms and over wide periods of time: in fact, it is less a matter of the history of costume itself, than of its social function in a changed world with new factors determining it."

With the Greeks, as during the Roman Empire, a style lasted for centuries. Prior to the Christian era, it took fifty years at least for a particular taste to cause a definite revolution. During the reign of royalty, fashion was changed more at the whim of a king or his mistress than for political or economic reasons with the exception of the French Revolution, and practically at every season, a new style makes its appearance. The moving waistline rises, falls again, narrows, disappears. Shoulders become square-cut or sloping, sleeves cling, bulge out or disappear. The thigh shows itself a little, a lot, seductively, or not at all !

Revolutions also Take Place in the Female Body

How striking also are the variations in the feminine silhouette throughout the ages ! It would seem that the human body can be made to comply to the dictates of fashion (or to the preferences of men

*The beard is one of the conquests
of the new spirit.
It is no longer
the apanage of original men
harebrained
and people with bad manners.*

perhaps ?) At the height of their civilization, the Greeks had a preference for well-proportioned women, neither fat nor thin, high-breasted, with rounded hips and narrow waists. Statues are proof of this: the fair sex seems to be poured into the same mould, a mixture of harmony and majesty.

In Egypt today, as in all Middle-Eastern countries, we see fat women, with heavy breasts and thick thighs. Yet, in the time of the Ptolemies, they seemed to identify themselves with men by their drawn-out silhouettes, wide shoulders, small breasts and flat hips ! Yet one cannot accuse the Egyptian fresco-painters of being dishonest, for they faithfully reproduced everything they saw... sometimes even certain malformations !

If one were to photograph, one upon another, a score of these Greek statues or Egyptian bas-reliefs, as is sometimes done in order to reveal the basic "type" of a single family, one would obtain some very different types of women.

In Flanders or in France in the 15th century, the breast resembled a small apple, the neck was long and the stomach promising. In the 16th century, the bosom disappeared all over Europe, seemingly poured into a funnel. In the 17th century, Rubens and Jordaens show us some very buxom women, brimming over with pink flesh; Boucher and Watteau reveal us their physical charms, less generous perhaps, but comfortable enough nonetheless.

In 1925, the bosom was no longer fashionable, whether in France, Italy, Spain, or in North or South America. Ten years later it timidly rose over a tight waist. In 1940, the war flattened it once more. It is growing again since 1965... It is even advised to fill out the sweater, but to be more discreet when the moon is up... Poor bosom, it does its best !

The hip problem is a more complex one. It would seem that every pound gained chooses that very spot to settle, and none other. Hence the numerous methods employed to reduce it, such as localized sweating, appropriate exercises and vibromassage applied to those fleshy parts with which the Callipygian Venus seems so pleased ! Just try and make head or tail of all this !

The long and short of it is that the shape of a woman's body follows the fashion, as if by mere willpower one could inflate it or flatten it out like some rubber toy. It is the reflection of its age.

The First Department Stores

The first drapery stores opened under the arcades of the Palais Royal in Paris about 1805. "Little Nanette", followed by "Maid of Honor", "Little Red Riding-Hood", "The Vestal", "The Magic Lamp", "The Unfaithful Page" and "The Magots", were among the most frequented in 1825. "The Poor Devil" was still in existence in 1914. "The window-display and the shop-sign of a drapery shop are sources of cons-

Beards and skirts blossom and broaden.
(From left to right):

Little boys' jackets in 1830 were shorter than father's, but the trousers were the same.

Long hair and curly beards, circa 1840.

The extravagant shirts of the late 1800s were matched by the complicated hairdoes of ringlets, knots and chignons.
(Carnavalet Museum.)

(From left to right):

A portrait of Maria Volkonska also shows a glimpse of the Chita Prison in Siberia. (Pushkin Museum Leningrad.)

Boys and girls in 1830.

Plumed hats and curls in 1830.

Parisian dresses of 1830 were worn with tulle butter-muslin turbans and merino cloaks.

Costumes and coiffures considered appropriate for visiting in the country, circa 1830.

Styles for the city girl in 1830.
(Carnavalet Museum.)

t do girls dream of ?

tant care and attention on the part of the shrewd shop-keeper: huge brightly colored bands take up the entire shop front. The abundance of wares must be such (at least to outward appearances) that one can scarcely squeeze between the counters. It would be ridiculous to advertize less than twenty-five thousand dresses at one and the same time." So Montigny tells us in his book "A Provincial in Paris", in 1825.

Even after Napoleon's abdication, women went on wearing dresses tightly gathered beneath the bosom and around their thighs, and this in spite of being nicknamed "broomsticks" by the journalists. Yet this model inspired the elegant winter "Russian Witzchouras", a kind of furlined sheath with sleeves extending down over the wrists in *mittens*.

Wigs were still curly and the humblest woman would have blushed at the thought of going to a ball with her own hair. Those who could not afford a complete wig, bought a "front twist" or else a chignon (like our present-day daughters of Eve). Having to make do without permanent waves, they puffed out their hair over steaming water.

The Restoration did not bring any great changes in fashion. Leroy had turncoated at the right moment, and, by replacing the Imperial eagles on his shop front with fleurs-de-lys, he considered that he had paid his debt to the Monarchy. His style became more discreet, however. Values had changed. The nobles who had returned to France caught up with the fashion, but with moderation. Duchesses and

1832, " Romantic sleeves are like balloons filled with air," states Lady's Magazine,

" in case of shipwreck, they can be used as a life buoy ! "

grouchy old nobles looked disdainfully upon the bourgeois and this new aristocracy with its faulty speech and colorful phraseology. But it must be admitted that these female upstarts were beautiful and most elegant. "Their little hands, cleverly made white, handle glove and fan with a very French gracefulness. They have astonishing chic and smartness," according to a Paris chronicler. A curious phenomenon then took place. Not wishing to be outdone by the good taste displayed by the old aristocracy, the new rich were determined to prove that they too had "class". And as the nobles tried to show their elegance by means of subtle refinements, everyone gradually found a common level.

During Louis XVIII's time, smart men wore French-style dress with trousers tightly fitting right down to the shoes or cut out at the instep. Short trousers with white stockings, a plain waistcoat and a frock-coat stiffened with five collars one on top of the other were also current. The use of these clothes differed according to the years, the quality of the cloth, the shape of the tails, the color of the waistcoat or the design of the buttons.
Hats, made of melusine, had deep and flared crowns. There were two innovations however: the opera hat, or "crush" hat, invented in 1823 and perfected by Monsieur Gibus, and the overcoat, much decried to begin with, but later adopted because of its convenience.

Lord Spencer unwittingly Started a Fashion

The spencer, as leeved bolero, first made its appearance in England, after the Revolution, in a very amusing manner. Lord Spencer, London man about town who was very fond of the bottle, fell asleep one day with his back to the fire, so close to the embers that he burnt the tails of his frockcoat. He was so angry at this accident, that he had the burnt ends cut off immediately and walked out into the street. Believing that he was launching a new fashion, some eccentrics immediately ordered themselves "Spencer jackets". A few years later, French women adopted this style and wore a jacket over their dress.
Feminine waists, though still high, became a little thicker, as women — who were crazy about furbelows — trimmed the hems of their dresses and their necklines with ruching, plumes, little lace frills and ribbons. Their sleeves gradually puffed out more and more, a forestate of the famous "leg of mutton" sleeves.

The Fashion Was Romantic

In 1825, an intellectual movement of the "romantic" type had such an influence on dress as to transform it by stages. Youth seemed to lose interest in money and the ostentation which had inspired the maddest eccentricities during the first revolutionary upheavals. Music and poetry counterbalanced the middle-class tendency. Byron, Walter Scott, Liszt

" The world is a gambling game in which all is confused.   One person believes he has won when often he loses.   Mathurin Regnier

and Chopin charmed the Restoration. Lady Morgan wrote in *La France :* "All that is English is now the fashion in Paris and thereby romantic. We have tailors, dressmakers, pastry shops and even doctors and apothecaries, and all of them romantic."

The lady of fashion had to be languishing; she fainted at the least provocation, be it a perfume too strong or a word out of place. In order to remain slim, she secretly drank vinegar, shortened her nights and refused all food. She was practically dying of starvation. In order to revive herself whenever she had "vapors", she kept a bottle of smelling salts close at hand, or attached to her ring. She had to be dressed with a certain carelessness. One went out in the street without a hat, with one's hair falling down to one's shoulders in thick curls called "repentances". No powder or rouge, only a cambric handkerchief in one's hand, ready to wipe away a tear which might be provoked at any moment by some sight offensive to one's sensibility.

One dreamed in the moonlight and committed suicide because of an unhappy love affair... When reading books of that period, we are reminded of present-day scenes.

A man, in order to be up to date, "should, at first glance, offer the spectacle of sickness and unhappiness, with a little something neglected about his person, his beard neither whole nor shaven, but as though grown suddenly in a moment of surprise... Locks flying in the wind, a profound, sublime, distracted look, fatalistic, with lips contracted in disdain for the human species, bored at heart, drowned in disgust and the mystery of his being." This is Chateaubriand speaking.

Those charming young people had known, long before us, Grecomania. Past fashions were revived and beautiful women could be seen wearing a jewel on their foreheads in the "Belle Ferronnière" manner, a hair-style in the Sévigné manner and a skirt in the "Montespan" manner.

The names given to materials and colors vied with each other in extravagance. A rather light green was called "love-sick toad", a darker shade of green "startled toad"; a pale-grey velvet was on the market called "frightened mouse" and a darker grey taffeta: "spider meditating a crime". As for the new materials, these were called "poplin", "zinzolin", "stokolmie", "canezou", "bazazinkoff".

Skirts remained long, but became bell-shaped. Belts slowly descended to the waist. Shoulders appeared to droop as sleeves were fitted very low and became so voluminous that it took a steel framework to prevent them from sagging... they were reminiscent of the Renaissance. In this connection, the "Lady's Magazine" of 1832 describes — with a flash of English humour — those romantic sleeves as "air-filled balloons which could, if necessary, be of use in a shipwreck" ! Of course, "Mae Wests" had not yet been invented.

Fashion details changed with increasing rapidity and "Ladies" journals sprang up on all sides to explain them.

Hairstyles became a dashing combination of smoothed curls and flowers, paradise feathers, ears of corn and beribboned flounces, the whole gathered in a bun on top of the head and embellished with curls over the temples. But, unfortunately, bonnets grew proportionately — a less happy development. Large

turbans were very much in fashion and gave women a slightly Oriental look reminiscent of the Middle Ages. One hairstyle was inspired by the giraffe offered by the Egyptian pasha to Charles X in 1827. This noble mammal, installed at the Jardin des Plantes, received more visitors than the King. The hairstyle bearing its name, however, was not a very tall one. It consisted of a thick plait twisted around the head in the Russian style and topped with a series of curls. A flat hairstyle in the Chinese manner was also popular for a time.

Corsets slowly reappeared, smaller and more discreet, intended to reduce the waist, but without stiffening the entire silhouette. Flexible ones in the "lazy" style were made for informal wear in the mornings, and others fitted with "pulleys" enabled one to lace or unlace them without help...

Little by little, the very tight waist, worn with skirts which gradually became wider and considerably shorter, gave women a fragile appearance which became more apparent as time went by. With her flat shoes, her embroidered openwork stockings, her V-shaped décolleté and her vaporous dresses, the coquette of Charles X's reign had a charm all of her own, precious and rather like a "doll in a shop window". Unfortunately the hairstyle also increased in size and its balance necessitated seven combs, one of which was a dress comb !

Monsieur Plaisir, inventor of curled plumes, and Monsieur Croizat, "hairdressing's Napoleon", thought up — as in Marie-Antoinette's days — hairstyles inspired by a fashionable book, painting or play... Masked balls were very popular and recalled the charms of a past age.

The aristocracy and the nobility are portrayed here in all their splendor.
(left to right):
Hélène Louise Elisabeth, Princess of Mecklenburg, as painted by Winterhalter.

Guests at a concert given in honor of Queen Victoria in the Guise Gallery of the Château d'Eu. (September 4, 1843.)

Dames Sociétaires of the Comédie Française in 1855.

Young Queen Victoria (1843), holding a flower and wearing a garter on her arm as painted by Winterhalter.

Andrieux reading in the Comédie Française in 1847. (Versailles Museum.)

Victorine and Palmyre were the smart dressmakers of the day. Stendhal mentioned the former in his "Memoirs of an Egotist"; it was from the latter that Eugenie de Montijo ordered some fifty-two different outfits designed to dazzle Napoleon III when she married the Emperor in 1853.

This brings us to the period 1830-1840 which was the height of femininity. Of course, hats were still too bulky, adorned with too many plumes, but from 1833 onwards they became more discreet, more delicately amusing. Although their crowns remained high, their brims framed the face and were tied beneath the chin with big colored bows. Locks falling on either side of the face were reminiscent of the hairstyle dear to the Marquise de Sévigné.

The dress, which was tightly fitted over a narrow body, spread out in the most charming manner to reveal tiny feet clad in buskins. The coquette's parasol was as sharply pointed as a sword and her handkerchief of fine cambric was edged with lace. It was during this period that the "grisette", charming ancestor of our "midinette" (young milliner-girl) appeared, both of which have held a very special place in Paris history due to their charm, grace, youth

Hats of the 1840 permitted but a dim view of the world.
(left to right):

This caricature was published in 1840.

A natty man's costume of 1840.

Another caricature of the popular style depicted the front view.
(Carnavalet Museum.)

(From left to right):

Ladies' shoes slim and pointed, circa 1840.

Sportive costumes, circa 1840.

These two noble ladies were portrayed by the court painter, Franz Winterhalter. (Versailles Museum.)

Tsarina Alexandra Feodorovna, wife of Nicholas I, was painted in a red dress. (Pushkin Museum, Leningrad.)

CHAUSSURES de DAMES.

and natural elegance. "The grisette," said a contemporary writer, "walks on her toes, swings her hips, keeps her stomach in, lowers her eyes, lightly nods her head and takes great pains to avoid splashing her fine white stockings with mud. She spends her youth painfully earning 30 sous a day, 574.50 Francs per month."

George Brummell, First London Dandy

Louis-Philippe was a middle-class king and being middle-class was very much in favor at that time. The bourgeois was rich and showed it. His dress was flashy and his wealth was showy. Once again British "good taste" was to impose its elegant discretion via George Brummell, the first London dandy who seems to have been conceived and brought into the world for that very purpose. He maintained that "if the people stare at you, it means you are not well dressed." (How true, but this did not prevent him from ruining himself and dying at Caen at the age of 62.)

The necktie became the main focal point of the cos-

tume. Brummell, who spent two hours dressing every day, sacrificed a great deal of time to this detail. "He replaced soft muslin with a slightly starched material..." we are told by a contemporary writer. "Standing before his mirror, he reduced his tie to more reasonable dimensions by the soft and gradual pressure of his lower jaw. The shape of each successive fold was given to it by the collar of his shirt which he had just turned down." Faced with such difficulties, it is no wonder that Honoré de Balzac should have published under the pen-name of "Baron de l'Empesé" (Baron Starch) a booklet entitled: *The Art of Putting on One's Tie in Eighteen Lessons.*

With the help of George IV and a few friends, Brummell launched a suit of impeccable cut, fitted to perfection in a formal style tinged with insolence. It consisted of a coat with long flaps, a buttoned waistcoat and trousers tightly fitting down to the ankle for town wear, or suede breeches fitted into short boots for the country. The tophat, square and flat was as indispensable to the gentlemen of those days as the bowler-hat is today to London bankers. The French snob of 1840 thus had to become a sportsman,

For the man of today, the hat is not a necessary headcovering.

For the man of the 19th century, the hat was an insignia, an

emblem, a talisman as well as an indication of his standing.

a lover of horses and affect a trace of English accent on the tip of his tongue.

It is curious to note that while male fashions were changing, journals ceased to take an interest in them and devoted themselves almost exclusively to the transformation in feminine attire.

Trousers Made a Timid appearance

In those days, fashionable women were called "lionesses". They had a cavalier provocative appearance, tossed off steaming punch or iced champagne, drew sword and pistol, rode horseback and were not afraid of smoking cigars and even wearing trousers! French law however forbade women to wear trousers (both literally and figuratively speaking) and the small number of eccentrics who tried to ignore the law became subject to such unpleasant curiosity that very quickly the only ones to adopt this garment were maids (of easy virtue).

Naturally, the "lionesses" brought "lions" in their wake, idle and charming, impeccably dressed and wearing long hair in the Alfred de Musset style, and melusine top-hats.

The upheavals of 1848 were to speed aside once and for all these cardboard carnivores to make way for two new categories of madcaps: the "rowdies" and the "mysterious ones". The former category affected an air of irresponsibility, whereas the latter were recognizable by their affected air of nobility and reserve.

(From left to right):

A style of 1855 as painted by Van den Hout. (Carnavalet Museum.)

The crinolined dress was adapted for a side-saddle riding costume. This illustration is dated August, 1861. (American Library, Paris.)

" The stallion is the image of mocking friend : he neighs under every horseman."   The Koran

THE ELEVENTH REVOLUTION

THE AGE OF THE CRINOLINE

From the very outset of Napoleon III's reign in 1852, the whole western world was influenced by the fashions created in France. Their impact was to be so enduring that henceforth France would be the arbiter of elegance throughout the world.

Needless to say, this pace-setting country was able to profit from the technical and industrial innovations achieved elsewhere in the world.

The sewing-machine had greatly improved since its invention in 1830 by a Frenchman, Barthélemy Thimmonier. In 1846, an Englishman, Elias Howe discovered a way of making his machine sew on both sides of the material by means of two threads, one above the other. Isaac Singer, an American, patented a similar machine in 1851 and was promptly sued for patent infringement by Howe who won his case. Singer had to pay a twenty-five dollar fine on each sewing machine for the next 25 years... nevertheless

he had made these machines available for all pocket-books.

A few years later, the United States came up with a shoe-making machine enabling mass-production of shoes, and a mechanical-embroidering loom which scallopped, hem-stitched and produced open-work embroidery more economically than by hand. A machine which cut several layers of material at the same time was invented in 1854. Another appeared in 1867 which cut and stitched button-holes, and finally in 1900, appeared one which sewed on the buttons themselves. The textile industry had never known such activity. The variety and perfection of figured cloths developed in the most incredible way. Brocaded satins, marbled velvets flowered taffetas, glossy moires, woollen gauzes printed with little flowers all made their appearance. Striped and printed fabrics were also produced.

By discovering new methods of dyeing and new dyes, chemists provided manufacturers with new possibilities unheard of up until that day. Artificial indigo was invented by a French chemist, Jean Guimet in 1826, fuchsine was discovered in 1856, and synthetic

(From left to right)

London ladies in June 1863 were wearing spring gowns. (American Library, Paris.)

A carriage-rental sign of the mid-19th century. (Carnavalet Museum.)

Frills and flounces trimmed the skirts of London ladies in May, 1861. (American Library, Paris.)

More than ever, woman takes the defensive, protecting herself

either by advances or by strongly protected rear positions.

Not an inch of skirt was bare of decoration as we see in the following gowns in 1873, in 1875 and in 1877.
(Carnavalet Museum.)

183

indigo in 1876. It is worth noting that these new colors were not very fast, requiring a constant renewal of materials, consequently of styles, at an ever accelerated rate.

This budding textile industry forced Europe to augment its importation of silk, wool and cotton. At the time of the American Civil War, England was purchasing 70 % of the American cotton crop. Gradually also a ready-to-wear clothing industry was developing.

The Invention of "Sales"

Gradually small shops expanded into department stores. The Louvre opened its doors in 1885, and three years later produced its first catalogue. The Printemps was opened in 1865, and the Galeries Lafayette in 1895.

Such stores, as they developed the art of displaying their products began to exert a real fascination upon the fair sex. When the Bon Marché, built in 1851 was moved to Rue de Sèvres, its actual address, in 1869, the annual turnover was twenty million gold francs. But the invention of the sale midcentury was the great revolution in the lives of women. This method proved so attractive to some women that they would come home in the evening having spent a fortune on "bargains". Others spent entire days selecting articles which they were to reject the following day. The "shop-psychosis" was born.

" She wavers, she hesitates, in short, she is a woman."

Racine

One wonders where and how they sat down in costumes suckar. (left to right):

these Opera gowns of 1871;

these red evening dresses of 1860;

in these light blue evening dresses of 1860;

in this green and beige gown adorned with artificial roses of 1875. (Carnavalet Museum.)

THE FIRST CRINOLINE

These fancy faibelowed gocons were created in Paris between 1873 and 1877.
(Carnavalet Museum.)

Crinolines first made a timid appearance around 1845. At first they were worn over a simple petticoat made of horsehair canvas. Later, around 1850, this petticoat was reinforced with whalebone and metal strips all around the lower part of the skirt except the front forcing the skirt to balloon out in the back. As the crinolines gradually widened, they became known as the cage, a bulkier petticoat skirt which assumed the shapes of balloons, sacks and barrels and was worn beneath dresses with several tiers of flounces.

Bodices, close-fitting with little pointed collars came right up to the neck and were decorated with cloth or Brandenburg lace.

Around 1854, pagoda-type sleeves and bracelets were replaced by slashed sleeves while the burnous coat, first worn during the reign of Louis-Philippe at the time of the Algerian conquests was superceded by the overcoat with back flaps longer than those in front. Fitted close to the bodice, it was embellished with a tiny cape called a "jockey".

One of the most important parts of feminine attire at that time was the mantlet or short cloak nearly always trimmed with a wide lace flounce or tasselled fringe. There was also the "kasawekas", a kind of little cassock ending below the waist.

At the same time, coats were often replaced by big fringed shawls while veils became much smaller. "Cabriolet" hats remained fashionable, swallowing up the nape of the neck with their enormous crowns and hiding the throat with wide ribbons tied beneath the chin. Hair styles on the other hand were charming with their bandeaux and bunches of curls gathered over the temples which were decorated with flowers in the evening.

Refinement in dress was the key word even among the *demi-mondaines* who cultivated an air of luxury without ostentation. Concealed beneath a seemingly well-to-do middle-class façade could be seen such well-known names as "La Belle" Castiglione who, in the privacy of her home, entertained her friends clad only in an animal skin, and Madeleine Borhan whose crinolines were so wide that double doors had to be opened whenever she stepped onto the stage at the Comedie Française.

In another two years, the whole of French womanhood would wear only crinolines... how did such an extravagant skirt come to be so popular? Possibly because of Eugenie, wife of the emperor, Napoleon III. The Second Empire greatly modified the life and fashions of France. Even though Napoleon was sometimes called the "melancholy parrot",

his Court was luxurious. Receptions and balls were frequent, and the Empress, a devilish coquette, spent a fortune on her clothes, especially those created by the English couturier, Charles Worth.

Eugenie adored crinolines. Why? Perhaps because she wanted to hide her legs? This reason is unlikely for she was known to have pretty legs, and liked to show them off, as did all the beauties of the Court, as they mounted their carriages. Probably the Empress favored them because these outsized skirts flattered the bust, and the wide neckline. Above this, the head rose like a rose and the waist seemed become even slimmer. Naturally the Court influenced the town and the town influenced the country and so a new era of fashionable follies was launched.

The crinoline made a good deal of ink flow in those days. Some found the form fairylike; others uttered indignant cries. Others found it amusing while still others saw evidences of eroticism.

BAUDELAIRE LOVED CRINOLINE

Baudelaire, speaking of the women of the Second Empire, wrote, "Women perform a kind of duty in trying to appear magic and supernatural; they must surprise and beguile".

Yet these petticoat skirts were not favored by all. Gyp, the pen name for the Countess de Martel de Janville, was horrified when as a little girl she saw them at the races at Auteuil. "Women climbed on chairs to watch the horses," she wrote in her memoirs. "It was just like a sea of tossing cages showing off legs which appeared to me to be short and heavy. Underclothes beneath the cages were varied. Some were frothy, a real foam of muslin and lace; others were severe or strict or just easy-going and amusing." It would seem that the underwear of the Second Empire was most full of fancy.

How can we adequately imagine the kicks

which these delightful creatures

accomplish with such a flourish,

thus twisting their trains and freeing the space.

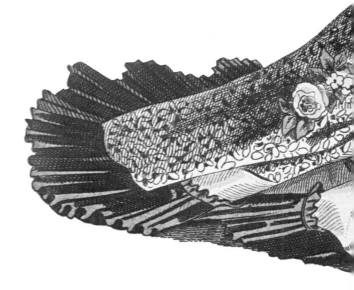

(From left to right): a concert toilet, 1873.

A dress from the Maison Tainturier, 1875.

An elegant woman of 1877.

Fashions of 1877. (Carnavalet Museum.)

189

Dress designers, both men and women create many beach toilets

but they so strongly resemble visiting dresses

that one is confused.

"Hooped crinoline seems also to possess a symbolic meaning," wrote a Dutchman. "If we consider this bulky garment in relation to the characteristic conditions of the period as a whole, it seemed to be an expression not so much of woman's triumph but rather of her inaccessible loneliness. The foot, no longer visible to the eye, became a source of all kinds of erotic fancies. Indeed women paid particular attention to their shoes as if wishing to stimulate these fancies, but sheltered by their crinolines, they still retained every appearance of virtuousness."

It is odd how these crinolines fired the imagination. Another book published in Paris in 1826 was entitled, *The Art of Lifting One's Dress*. This manual showed a hundred ways of playing with hoops... and of displaying adorable little button boots scarcely reaching the ankle. In any case a great deal of gracefulness and skill was required to move about in homes of that period, crowded as they were with knick-knacks and small pieces of furniture. Impulsive movements were well-nigh impossible.

In 1867, a new fashion appeared on the Parisian boulevards: elegant ladies wore lace-edged ruffs around their ankles. These latest follies were attached to a long wide pair of pants which were in turn attached to the waist by a string. Where did such a garment come from? Quite simply from the drawers worn in the 18th century by dancers, ice-skaters and servants in order to protect their modesty in case of a fall. However, despite its possible benefits, the Parisians quickly gave up this pantaloon which right-thinking people found offensive simply because of its suggestive powers. Right-thinking people apparently had evil minds. And so, once again, pantaloons were reserved for little girls and prostitutes!

CHARLES WORTH INVENTS LA RUE DE LA PAIX

In 1845 a talented young Englishman full of daring arrived in Paris with seventeen francs in his pocket. Charles Frederick Worth dreamed of fashion and success. In 1858, he set up business on Rue de la

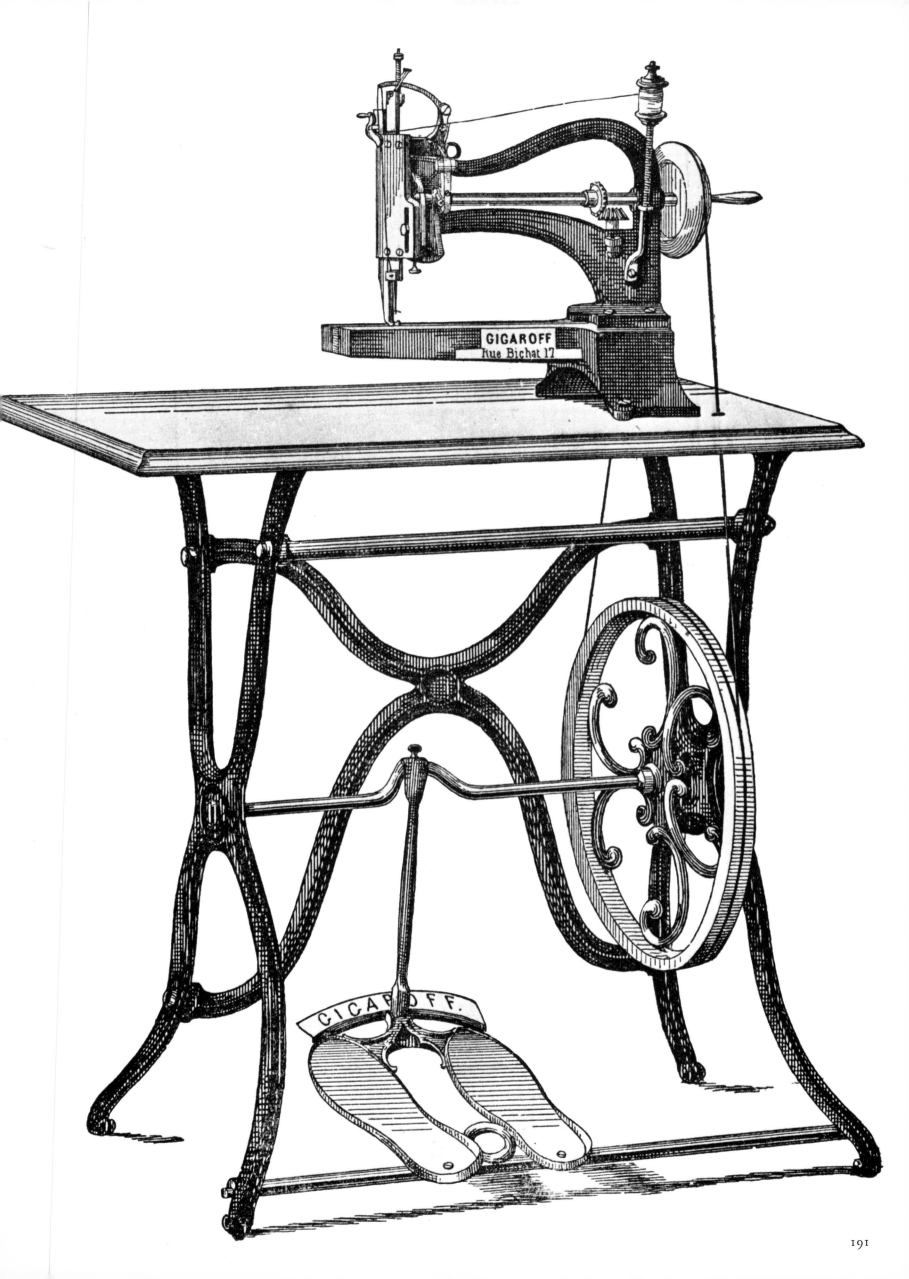

GIGAROFF
Rue Bichat 17

GIGAROFF.

" Do not be mistaken, bad company corrupts good habits."   *St. Paul*

The gowns of the late 19th century lent themselves well to the romantic interpretation of France's impressionist painters.
(left to right):

" Le Moulin de la Galette " by Renoir.

"Women in the Garden" by Claude Monet.

" Monsieur et Madame Bernheim de Villers " by Renoir.

" Madame Darras " by Renoir.
(Jeu-de-Paume Museum.)

Paix. By 1860, his fame was such that the Empress Eugenie became his client. Rue de la Paix had arrived, and after that famous women the world over would do anything in order to be dressed by him. Worth was invited into the best homes, and as a fashion-designer was accepted as the equal of a talented musician or composer. Worth soon came to regard himself as the equal of a king. and received his customers in like manner, according to one description: "Women will go to any lengths to be dressed by him. He receives them reclining on a divan, cigar in his mouth and tells them, 'Walk ! Turn around ! Very well, come here, I will compose your outfit for you.' It was not they who would choose but he ! " It was even necessary to have an introduction in order to be served by him.

Once a lady of high society came to order a gown. "Madame, by whom were you recommended ?"

"What do you mean ?"

"It is necessary to have an introduction in order to be dressed by me."

The lady left in a dungeon.

To the people who were shocked by his behaviour he answered, "I am a great artist. I have the color sense of Delacroix and I create. A gown is worth a painting. Art is God and the bourgeoises are made to take our orders."

Second Empire hair styles underwent three changes: during the first of these (1852-1860), hair came down to the neck or over the shoulders. Bonnets were tied like hoods and had a short curtain behind. During the second change (1860-1885), hair styles were to climb upward, making hats heavier as a result. The third change which lasted until the war of 1870 found hair piled on top of the head with curls coming down into the nape of the neck.

Hats were considered to be indispensable. In 1860 Caroline Reboux set up a millinery business in the Rue de la Paix. Her name remained a symbol of perfection right up until the Second World War when women finally gave up wearing hats. Necklines bared the shoulders. Collars of varying widths covered the shoulders and the tops of the arms. Great cape-coats covered the whole dress. Hoods lost their cuffs and became a sort of bonnet tied by ribbons under the chin.

Rising wages entailed high prices and instead of paying 18 pounds for frothy undies of muslin, the ladies now paid 25 pounds for them, and 15 pounds for underskirts — even in the department stores.

LADIES GO BATHING

"As early as 1829, ladies were seen to go bathing in wide trousers, tightly fitted at the ankle and two-colored jackets with long sleeves," wrote Madame Deslaudes in her *Five Thousand Years of Elegance*. "This costume called the 'zouave' was made of wool serge or white piqué and trimmed with braid. A little linen corset without whalebones was worn beneath and one entered the water in black stockings and ankle-length boots made of canvas with metal soles." In 1889, bathing costumes became dressier still with pleated trousers beneath a pleated skirt and a long tight-fitting jacket with buttons. Sleeves were short and the wide square collar was tightly tied beneath the chin with a big bow.

BIRTH OF THE COCODETTE

The exhibition of 1867 brought Spanish fashion to Paris. A crinoline supported skirt, though less bulky than the current French style, was topped by a little bolero and a small hat perched over the forehead. Gradually women grew "narrower" and also more masculine with their jackets decorated with Brandeburg lace. Hats had upturned brims and were ornamented with cock-feathers or ostrich plumes. Their fur-lined coats were reminiscent of those worn by the grenadier guards. The new skirts were slightly shorter and lifted up in back making their wearers look rather like hens — hence their nick-name of "cocodettes". The male escorts of these ladies were called " petits crevés" or fops.

The war of 1870 was to put an end to crinoline once and for all but women still refused to return to a completely plain shape following the lines of the body. They adopted a "dress-improver", a kind of cage placed in the small of the back and used to support the "bustle" beneath which all the fullness of the skirt was gathered. It was distinctly reminiscent of the fashion which preceded the French Revolution. These gowns were loaded with trimmings, a style typical of this era. The "upholstery look" which was all the rage in apartments with their decor of tassels, ruchings and paddings, had spread all the way into fashion. It was nothing but drapery from skirts to curtains. Simplicity was definitely out of favor and homes were crazy places, stuffed with objects, carpets, poufs and plants.

FIRST TAILORED SUIT LAUNCHED
BY REDFERN

Redfern like Worth was English, and like him fought his first battles in London. Redfern however was specialized in tailoring and, in 1885, was the first to make the tailored suit which is to this day an essential element in our wardrobes. A plain skirt and matching jacket were combined with a waist-coat or blouse of a different color and cloth.

These couturiers were not content as they are today to show only two collections a year. Instead they created special models for their clients throughout

" For the unfortunate, for those in a hurry
who have neither fortune
nor sufficient patience to turn to the services of a tailor,
a sole resource : ready-made."

"From the very source of pleasure
rises something indescribably bitter which,
down to the flowers, takes you by the throat."
Lucretia

the year. Thanks to this system, each elegant woman in 1850 was able to have a highly personal style of dressing. In previous periods, fashion had either been dictated or rejected by the Court, according to the whims of the reigning monarch and his ladies. But in this period, a designer like Jacques Doucet could design vaporous dresses for the actress Réjane which were as reminiscent of the past as the suits of Redfern forecast the future.

THE CORSET RETÚRNS

Once again, waists were to be strangled. Women almost squeezed themselves to death in order to gain an inch. The necessity for this was explained in a little English book, *The Art of Learning to Correct Nature* with all the seriousness of the British. The author invites mothers to supervise the corseting of their daughters with a sadistic refinement similar to that of the Chinese who maimed their daughters' feet to keep them small. As a result hips swelled out and so did bosoms. Poor women! They were turned into a sack of oats tied in the middle. The corset, which was tightened with the help of the knee, turned the chubbiest woman into a wasp. The chest was choked and deformed by compression — no matter! Polaire, the most popular actress of the day, had a waist measurement which did not exceed 20 inches and everyone tried to imitate her at all costs. Despite these extremes wrought by corseting, fashion as a whole had a distinctly middle-class look, which was a result of the influence of France's new republicain government.

THE END OF THE BUSTLE

In 1889, the Eiffel Tower was born and with it a new style. Women did away with their bustles, and adopted a fuller skirt. Outsized sleeves were attached high on the shoulder. Ruffles of all shapes revealed starched or boned shirt-fronts. Women now resembled well-rounded cabbages from which protruded a tiny head crushed beneath a Charlotte hat covered with plumes and gew-gaws.

Portraits of Parisian ladies were a favorite subject of artists of the day.
(left to right):

Madame Gaudibert as portrayed by Monet. (Jeu-de-Paume Museum.)

Madame Charles Max as portrayed by Boldini. (Museum of Modern Art, Paris.)

"Une soirée" by Jean Béraud. (Carnavalet Museum.)

A "Portrait of Honorine" was painted by Toulouse-Lautrec. (Jeu-de-Paume Museum.)

Jean Béraud painted a typical afternoon gathering in Paris' Café Gloppa.

Crossing the Place de la Concorde by Jean Béraud. (Carnavalet Museum.)

(From left to right):
Two styles of suits, 1908;
two styles of mustaches.
(Carnavalet Museum.)
Silhouettes of 1900.
On a café terrace, Paris,
1900.
Boni de Castellane presented the epitome of refined elegance.
(Bibliothèque Nationale.)

About 1900 the beard gave way for the mustache which became

It threatens the sky, curves into girandoles.

Bristling, rooled, wavy, curled, proud or discouraged, its language is universal.

WOMEN ARE FREED BY THE WAR

THE TWELTH REVOLUTION

DEATH OF THE CORSET

Before going on to describe the fashion explosion which took place in 1900, thanks to the fashion bombshell launched by the French couturier Paul Poiret, it is necessary to plunge the reader into the Parisian atmosphere of that period. Both extravagant and voluptuous, in which (so we are told) they knew the art of gracious living... But we should add straight away that those concerned were a small, a very small, *élite* who certainly gave no thought to paid holidays, or to ready-made clothes...

The international exhibition of 1900 was a major event in Paris and in the world. Tourists poured in, eager to take advantage of this unique opportunity, not only to see Paris (*gai Paris*, of course), but also its world-famous designers who had come together to exhibit their latest creations.

Thus Paris was still the center of the world. From all sides people came there to spend fortunes, to indulge in pleasure, to dress better than anywhere else, to find the most perfect elegance, the subtlest refinements.

Art Nouveau became the order of the day, with floral designs sweeping through fashion and doing away with the last vestiges of the bustle, replaced by " morning glory " skirts which rippled and wrapped themselves around the legs like some tropical plant, with a delightful rustle. Curiously enough, sleeves melted away like butter in the oven and light-weight materials replaced the heavy silks. The train reappeared, no longer sweeping behind, but " coiled " so as to show off the graceful silhouette and conform to the sinuous style. Unfortunately, hats grew

"What is important in life is not to have money but that the others have none."   *Sacha Guitry*

larger once again, and overflowed, recalling the plumed felts worn by musketeers of Louis XIV or the hoods worn by the Dukes of Burgundy at the end of the Middle Ages, but decorated with flower-bushes, clusters of egret feathers or silken paradise plumes.

The lady of 1900 was a far cry from her sister of 1800 who, buttoned up to the chin, seemed intrenched in her respectability. She discovered a taste for rounded curves and, at the same time, decided that life begins rather than ends at forty. " Passion " wrote a Frenchwriter at the beginning of this century, " is long-lived nowadays. "

Peaked Caps and Trousers for the Sportswoman of 1900
It is amusing to see how this new woman, keen as she was to wear overloaded hats, dresses with trains and to show off her wasp-waist, was also determined to keep up with the times, and took up sport. She wore woollen or linen tennis dresses (with a flannel acket to avoid chills) and not only showed herj ankles, but also her little feet shod with ghastly flat rubber-soled shoes !

Women cyclists wore cycling costumes : which were baggy bloomers (wide, but gathered in below the knee), a slim-waisted jacket over a ruffled blouse and a high collar.

(From left to right):

This illustration cartoons an exhibition of models in London. (Carnavalet Museum.)

"Woman in Blue" painted by Picasso, 1901. (Museum of Contemporary Art, Madrid.)

Portrait of Robert de Montesquiou, painted by Boldini. (Museum of Modern Art, Paris.)

Gambling in Monte-Carlo was cartooned by Sem. (Bibliothèque Nationale.)

"Beauties of the night", by J. Béraud. (Carnavalet Museum.)

" No one imagines how much wit is needed
not to be ridiculous."
Chamfort

Befurred and luxuriant was the spring fashion of 1910. (left to right):

(Carnavalet Museum.) Maria Guy's hat. (Bibliothèque Nationale.)

" Bare as a church wall.   Bare as an academician's speech."   Musset

Right-thinking newspapers such as " Fashion Illus-
trated " promptly published articles which revealed
a real indignation against these young people who
dared to flout public opinion and offend the bourgeois susceptibilities of that time.

" Up to now, we have tried to ignore ", said the
chronicler, " the fact that honest women - in a word,
homeloving women - who, in all circumstances, are
duly mindful and respectful of convention, should,
without blushing, appear in public wearing the costume you have seen and practice a sport which
the present generation loves to the point of madness."
And yet the fashion held good ! The ideal of every
"new-look" woman of the day no longer was only to
have chic but also "dash". The first automobiles
were to rouse passions. Kerosene-powered cars were
soon to compete against the "little queen" as the
bicycle was called. The Duchess of Uzès gloried in
the fact that she was the first woman to obtain a
driving permit and to risk her life in open racers
which tore down the roads at 30 m.p.h., and even
50 m.p.h. on the slopes...

These speed-fans covered their dresses or their skirts
with dust-coats, wore thick goggles over their eyes
and, since windscreens were not yet invented,
attached their hats with a colored muslin veil (pre-
ferably green) which they tied beneath the chin.

In the evenings, these coquettes generously revealed
their shoulders, fitted with fluttering flounces —
known as "trailers" — at the back. Their pointed
bootees, always buttoned up to the shin, peeped out

as discreetly as little mice poling their snouts out of
their holes. Jewels were in evidence to the point
of being ostentatious.

On the other hand, masculine fashions had changed
but little since the war of 1870, and England continued to set the pace. However, jackets were worn
more frequently and about 1875, the "suit" was
born : pants, jacket and vest of the same fabric. The
redingote was still used for formal wear, its length
differing with the years. Overcoats were fitted and
short, while in winter, a fur-lined wrap was de
rigueur for men, the fur also trimming the cuffs and
the collar.

In 1880, Englishmen were obliged to wear dinner
jackets in their clubs and at home, but this costume
relieved them of the necessity of wearing starched
dress shirts.

In 1895, trousers had a sharp crease ironed into
them and the length was shortened. Once again, it
was the British gentlemen who set this fashion for
the continent. The wits of the day quipped, "Pants
are shortened in Paris because it rains in London."
The "melon" hat appeared toward the end of the
Second Empire but was not to be considered as fit
for formal occasions. Top-hats remained the elegant
hat : shiny black for the evening and grey for the
races. The soft felt would not begin its successful
career until 1885. During the summer, the "Panama"
or the straw "boater" were preferred.

Let's also keep in mind that until the war of 1914,
men never took off their hats or their gloves either in

The changing fashion on the eve of World War I. (left to right):

Tired by the arduous chore of shopping, the ladies relax on the terrace of the Bon Marché, one of Paris' main department stores.

These afternoon dresses, circa 1913, have an old-fashioned look.

The Louvre, another department store, offered these styles on Monday, March 30, 1914.

Parisian chic as designed by "grand couturier" Lelong in 1913.
(Carnavalet Museum.)

There is a time for everything, a time for everything under the sun.

(From left to right):

"Gilles", a winter coat of beaver and gold cloth, bordered by white fox. (Bibliothèque Nationale.)

"Nini of the Folies-Bergères", as portrayed by Van Dongen about 1918. (Museum of Modern Art, Paris.)

This serge suit by Doucet featured a jacket with a velvet collar opening on a lawn vest worn over white lace chemisette. August 1913. (Bibliothèque Nationale, Paris.)

Muffled up to the nose in a fur cocktail, here is the first "femme fatale" of the century.

drawing rooms or at the theater. They even carried canes to the opera, providing that the cane was of Malacca without knots or topped by a stone or tortoise-shell head.

This was also the "Belle Epoque", that of the high-class courtesan whose species was to disappear with the 1914-1918 war. These extraordinary women, in whose company the crowned heads of Europe and the smartest aristocrats showed themselves and spent fortunes, were called Émilienne d'Alençon, "La Belle" Otero, Liliane de Pougy, Mademoiselle de Clomesnil (who acted as a model to Marcel Proust for Odette de Crécy) only to mention a few.

Proust was to speak of feminine costumes with the delight of a gourmet. He wrote, "She had a sharp profile and a too fragile skin, her cheekbones were too high and the features too pinched. Her eyes were beautiful but so big that they seemed to give way under their own weight...

"The forehead and the temples were covered by a mass of hair that was brought forward, lifted, teased and spread over the ears in wild curls; as to her body which was admirably made, it was difficult to follow its continuity as the bust blossomed out as over an imaginary stomach and finished abruptly in a point while underneath the balloon of double skirts began to swell out, giving the impression of a woman composed of different pieces badly joined together so independent of its line were the ruchings, the flounces and the gilet, the bows, foams of lace and fringes of jet which followed the length of the corset without being in any way attached to the person who found herself bundled up or lost within them.

"She was dressed beneath her mantilla (Odette de

The Chinese tame fowl by cutting their wings and women by deforming their feet.

A skirt around the ankles has similar effect."

(From left to right):

"Which ?" An evening dress by Paul Poiret in white and black liberty satin, embroidered with pearl roses, appeared in the September 1913 issue of the Gazette du Bon Ton.

"The new collar" by Paul Poiret had a black satin skirt lined with white. The silk tunic was bordered with black fox, and the sleeves pearled with diamonds and jet-glass. (Gazette du Bon Ton, Bibliothèque Nationale.)

Crécy) in a cascade of black velvet which was obliquely held up so as to show, in a wide triangle, the bottom of a white ribbed-silk skirt and revealed a patch, also of white silk, at the opening of the low-cut bodice into which was stuck a bouquet of cattleya flowers."

The Worth Sons, Maggie Rouff, Doeillet, Madame Chéruit, Paquin (whose speciality was to dress queens and who was the first to open a branch in London), the Callot sisters, friends of the Goncourts (who introduced the kimono-sleeve into France), Jacques Doucet; these were the ones who made the law in the world of fashion.

Madeleine Vionnet had a place apart in the Parisian couture. After a short period with the Callot sisters, then as a designer for Doucet, she opened her own house on rue de Rivoli in 1912. After the war, she advocated a personalized approach, the style adapted to each client. Her technique of using the bias of the cloth, her science of cutting made her a specialist of the "draped movement". "As women's tastes evolve", she said, "I try to compose new harmonies on a theme that must remain unchanging."

And Now Meet Paul Poiret, Fashion-King of the Day
It was at Doucet's that young Poiret was to gain his first stripes. He had genius and was to revolutionize fashion by bringing a new form of beauty to women, but his beginnings were difficult. "Sales-girls", he wrote, "took a wicked delight in humiliating and snubbing me. I made my first model for the fancy-goods department, a little cape of red cloth with strips of cloth cut out along the neckline, forming a lapel of grey crêpe-de-chine, with which it was lined. It was buttoned down the side with six enamel buttons. Four hundred samples of it were sold, in several colors... One morning", he continued, "I saw Réjane arrive in her horse-drawn carriage and ask for Monsieur Doucet, to whom she spoke of her forthcoming play, 'Zaza'. In her part, she was to

"It is but a step from the sublime to the ridiculous."

Napoléon

(From left to right):

Three dresses of 1914.

Practical fashion in 1914.
(Bibliothèque Nationale.)

wear a gorgeous, voluptuous coat, capable of moving and electrifying not only her former lover, opposite whom she played in her cabaret role, but also the entire audience. I was given the job of making it. After spending sleepless nights thinking about it, I finally did produce a coat. It was of black tulle over black taffeta hand-painted by Billotey (a famous fan-painter of that day) with huge mauve and white irises, a large mauve satin ribbon and another of violet satin running through the tulle, circling the shoulders and closing the coat in front with a fancy bow. All the sadness of a romantic ending was contained in this very expressive coat. From then on, my reputation was made both at Doucet's and in Paris. I had made a name for myself on the shoulders of Réjane."

As one can see, modesty was not one of young Poiret's strong points. He had a taste for luxury and his first salary of 500 francs was immediately converted into opal cuff-links signed by Cartier.

Two years later, he fell out with Doucet and joined Jean and Gaston Worth. His stay with them was a short one. One day he entered Gaston's office with these words: "You asked me to create a potato-chips department, which I have done. But this has filled the house with a strong smell of frying which appears to inconvenience a lot of people. I am therefore thinking of frying my chips elsewhere on my own account. Would you care to pay for my frying-pan?" Worth smiled ironically and bade him good luck.

He Became Established in the Faubourg Saint-Honoré
The new king of Paris, a lover of colors, did not hesitate to match the most unlikely shades, ruby and amethyst, fuschia and cornflower blue, evanescent pink and acid green.

"Corsets were still worn in those days," wrote Poiret in his memoirs. "I declared war on them. The last specimens of these detestable contraptions were

"There are women who tell you they are
not for sale and who would not accept a centime from you!
These are generally the ones who ruin you!"
Sacha Guitry

1913... Here ends in the enchantment of a spring night a carefree world of pleasures. The bloodiest of all wars is about to engulf

called 'sarrauts'. I had always known women encumbered with their 'assets' and anxious either to conceal them or to distribute them. But this corset divided them into two distinct humps. On the one hand, the bust, throat and breasts, on the other the entire rear-end, so that women found themselves divided into two lobes and looking as if they had a trailer in tow.

"I therefore recommended that the corset be abandoned in favor of the brassière. I freed the bust, but fettered the legs instead. Women complained that they could no longer walk nor climb into a carriage. Their lamentations all pleaded against innovation." One of Paul Poiret's triumphs was his creation for Raoul Dufy of a workshop in which Zifferlin, a chemist and expert in aniline dyes and various other processes of printing on cloth, reproduced on fabulous materials the watercolors of this master "with his tiny gestures, baby-faced and curly as a fair and pink archangel". Marie Laurencin and Dunoyer de Segonzac also worked for him.
Poiret revived the tunic in a most unexpected style, with a very high waist, and, as he objected to puffed-out hair, he launched a smoothed-down hair-style, held in place with a headband tightly fitting over

the forehead and decorated with a cluster of egret plumes for evening-wear.
Paul Poiret, who was steeped in Orientalism, found a favorable climate for the success of his creations in the enthusiasm which swept through Paris after the "first night" of Diaghilev's Russian ballet which was decorated by Léon Bakst. Having sumptuous tastes himself, Poiret gave splendid receptions — including that of the "thousand and second nights" — in his residence of the Faubourg Saint-Honoré. He did not hesitate to dress his models in bloomerskirts which opened down the side to reveal matching pants, tightly gathered above the knee. This idea was later taken up by Maggy Rouff in 1942 for pretty cyclists of the time, and by Dior in 1960 for hostesses' dresses. Poiret was to speak of them to American women in these words : "You first adopted the bloomer-skirt in the shape of pyjamas. Now you will wear it for lunch and you have variations on the same theme for wearing at dinner... the bloomer-skirt is inevitable."

The First Live Models Travelled Europe under Poiret
Poiret was the first, once again, to have the idea of sending his models on a tour of Europe : "It was not so much a question of taking nine models away on

an entire civilization.

a tour, but of bringing them back to Paris safe and sound," he wrote. "My trip had to be in the best of taste and my publicity largely depended upon the good behavior of these young ladies. We left in two automobiles, all the models wearing the same costume, a very Parisian uniform consisting of a blue serge suit and a comfortable reversible plaid coat in buff. On their heads they wore oilskin hats with an embroidered P. It was frightfully smart."

Poiret excelled in one-piece evening coats cut out of the most sumptuous lamés. He not only influenced fashion, but also artists and the theatre. He brought to life the silk manufacturers of Lyons, who had dozed off into degenerate colors, by ordering orange and lemon-colored crêpe-de-chine, and loud greens and violets. He ordered a sketch-album of his creations from Iribe and another from Claude Lepape. He dressed the entire peerage; he was king of Paris.

Poiret's talent and success were at their climax when the 1914 war broke out. The world crisis did not prevent women from dressing. Parisian women shortened their dresses out of all proportion with the fashion of the day and slit them down the sides in order to walk faster. It was literally a new step away from femininity.

Novelties of 1921
(left to right):

Summer fashion, 1923.

Women on a terrace.
(Bibliothèque Nationale.)

SHAPES
DISAPPEAR

The desire to forget the horrors,
the thirst for life after the nightmare of the war,

gave to the Twenties the rhythm of a frenzied carnival.

Paris department stores offered their customers frivolities designed to eradicate the memories of the war.
(left to right):

The Bon Marché advertised these dresses in 1922. (Bibliothèque Nationale.)

First novelties of 1920 at the Bon Marché.

Au Printemps sold this bonnet in 1919. (Carnavalet Museum.)

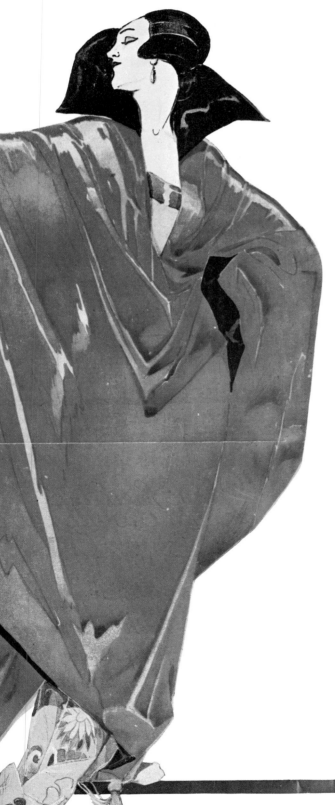

THE THIRTEENTH REVOLUTION

The tragedy of the First World War did not prevent women from being well-dressed. But, by force of circumstances, Parisian women became more discreet and practical.

Hair was worn in bands waved over the ears and boas and feathers draped and flew from head to toe. The tango was all the rage in the dances which were held all over Paris. Soldiers were on leave and must be amused... but to dance easily, shorter'looser skirts were necessary. Slowly the waistline inched toward the hips. Hats without brims were pulled firmly over the head and the bosom melted away as though ironed out of existence by a hot iron.

The Dolly Sisters launched a hairdo in the style of Joan of Arc. The French women came out of the 1914-1918 period with a pronounced taste for independence of thought and freedom of the body. The feminine standards of 1900 were brushed away into the dustbin. The waist was free.

The fashionable slogan became : "neither buttock nor nipple". The fair sex, obsessed with a slim silhouette, started to diet, wore strapped girdles and compressed their breasts with bandages. Waists settled at mid-thigh level.

The coiffure was, for a time, shaped into a "helmet"

"This delirious period thus takes its feverish colors."   *Paul Guth*

(From left to right):
Little girls' hats in 1925 copied the adult version. (Private collection.)

Spring furs in 1924 muffled ears and chins.

The Bon Marché department store proposed this meager silhouette for the winter of 1925. (Carnavalet Museum.)

In the Haute Couture world, Jeanne Lanvin made the silhouette of the period more interesting by embroidering leaf patterns on a silk lamé skirt. (Officiel de la couture.)

before finally being drawn back and shaved at the nape of the neck. Some preferred the style adopted by the Dolly Sisters with their hair combed stiffly over the ears and a big fringe eating into their eyebrows.

The waist descended to mid-thigh level over sleeveless tunics cut to just below the knee. Even the most select receptions took on the appearance of popular "hops", with shirt-dresses. Coats alone retained a certain elegance due to their luxurious fur trimmings. Shoes were pointed and had box heels. Straps over the instep became fashionable once again. For cocktails, pudding-bowl hats were crammed down to the eyebrows and ornamented with plumes — rather like feather-dusters — made of egret crests. This fashion for shirt-dresses, sack-coats and pot-hats was one of the least attractive we had known in centuries.

Women wore long earrings, pearl necklaces by the yard and bracelets studded with diamonds from wrist to elbow. Gold was no longer fashionable. It was worth less than platinum and four years of war and austerity invited ostentation.

Alongside the "nouveau riche" women, covered in jewels, there appeared the new dandies known as "petirs crevés", wearing skimpy jackets and trousers.

This was the period in which Colette, the unforgettable French writer on the foibles of women, wrote what turned out to be an accurate prophecy : "The time is perhaps not far off when the Haute Couture, creator of a kind of sumptuous indigence, will become alarmed at the results obtained. It makes it easy for anyone, with a capable pair of hands,

Already the little rabbit woman!

to cut a rectangle out of a piece of cloth, make two holes in it for the sleeves, and then allow the embroiderer, weaver or even painter to do his best on it. "Each time that the Haute Couture has created a severe design, and one so resembling a uniform that the color, ornamentation and consistency are what give it its character, and not its cut or design, she has light-heartedly foregone an important part of her prerogatives."

A certain Mademoiselle Coco Chanel was beginning to make a reputation for herself. It was whispered that she had started by selling sweaters out of a suitcase, but she now opened a fashion house where these same sweaters, of soft wool, chiné or camaïeu with matching crêpe-de-chine skirts were soon snatched up by all elegant women. Coco Chanel launched the little black dress and was very soon to become one of the great figures of Haute Couture. Meanwhile, Jeanne Lanvin was the one who enjoyed the most success with her picture-dresses, her personality and refined discretion, occasionally tinged with orientalism. Poiret carried on his revolutionary ideas with a zest and aggressiveness which were to kill him. Madeleine Vionnet, so feminine, re-invented the Greek drapé.

In 1917, Jean Patou was the first to import into France six American models! Dress-designers gradually gave up creating personalized dresses for individual clients, in favor of an extension into industrialization. Paquin launched the long-haired fur collar, turned up at the back and crossed over in front down to the waist. At the time, he was the undisputed king of fur and knew how to cut skins better than anyone else.

Lucien Lelong was a real magician and his evening gowns were spell-binding. It was not long before Christian Dior joined him as a designer. In 1931, there were many fashion houses in Paris. Besides the more important figures already mentioned, Molyneux was to have his period of fame when he dressed Marina of Greece, now Duchess of Kent. His creations were of a sober elegance. Auguste Bernard, Agnès Drecoll, Nicolle Groult, Prenet, Jeanne Regny were the fashionable designers of sportswear. Mainbocher dressed the Duchess of Windsor and created for her "Wallis blue".

O'Rossen, a specialist in tailored suits, "cut" English cloths to perfection. Every elegant woman owned one of his ensembles.

A trio of young couturiers was also making a name for themselves : Schiaparelli, Maggy Rouff and Marcel Rochas. All three were wonderful colorists and highly talented, though in very different directions. The first of these, Schiaparelli, dressed those in search of a wild touch. She launched the quilted evening cape and successfully harmonized pale blue and violet, emerald-green and ice-blue. The second, Maggy Rouff, had a refined sense of discreet Parisian elegance. Her shades were delightfully graded. The last, Marcel Rochas, inspired by a exhibition drawn from the colonies of the French empire, gave fashion an exotic touch which was to last for nearly fifteen years.

Four talented milliners created the most attractive hats for the entire world : Caroline Reboux, Rose Descat, Maria Guy and Jeanne Blanchot.

Sport became more and more fashionable and Hermès not only replaced the old-fashioned carpet-bag with valises of canvas edged with leather, but launched the zip-fastener and the ski-suit with leather jacket and drain-pipe ski-pants.

The genius of window display designed transformed the store fronts along the fashionable Faubourg Saint Honoré — and of the whole of France.

The years went by and the "green bean" style gave way to the "colocynth line"; the bosom reappeared (timidly), hips curved out (slightly) and the skirt stopped at mid-calf, revealing the gracefulness of the leg while concealing the so-often unattractive knee. Evening gowns once again became full-length with foulnced panels attached at mid-thigh level and wrapping themselves around the legs like convolvulus. The waist resumed its normal position, the neckline extended down the back to the waist, and shoulders were square. Fancy jewellery began a fabulous career; crystal necklaces were much sought after from then on.

In 1935, hats began to change. Losing their depth of crown, they began to curl up slightly at one side and eventually produced points sticking out on all sides. Some hats even hid one eye entirely; but in their efforts to be fashionable, elegant women gladly looked one-eyed. Then followed flat straw boaters, cosy hooded capes, pointed coolie hats, mob-caps in the "good little devil" style, caps with provocative peaks and minute berets stuck over the ear like a postage stamp on the corner of a letter. For evening wear, Agnes created flowered or

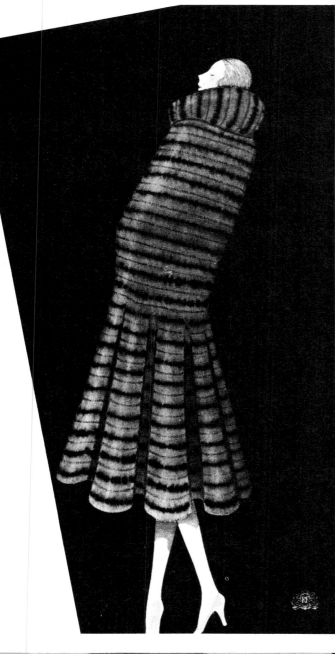

feathered hats or little cloth turbans to match the dress. Antoine, one of the master-hairdressers of the time, had great success with his reproductions of Queen Nefertiti's famous bandeau which he had admired in the Berlin Museum.

On the beaches, swimsuits at last dropped necklines and became shorter; beach pyjamas were all the rage. All of fashion was influenced by the Near East. Brandenburg braid made its appearance along with trouser-dresses in the Turkish style, Balkan braid and embroidery, Moroccan hoods, Cossack sleeves, and even a few 1880 bustles! Décolletés played truant from one shoulder to the other, slipped down between the breasts or lolled beneath the armpit...

In 1936 a small revolution occurred: the classic suit, neglected for the past ten years or so, made a very remarkable come-back in the form of a narrow skirt and severe jacket for morning wear. The popularity of restaurants and the success of the bistrots were to give this suit a position of honor. For evening-wear, it appeared cut out of fabric embroidered with colored arabesques, or in lamé or black velvet. It was worn with open-necked blouses in the sun-top style and made of satin or beautifully-worked crêpe, and was lined in matching material. The long-skirted costume also had its fervent adepts: O'Rossen, Creed, Knisé, Raphaël were the undisputed specialists of this new fashion.

Hair was worn long over the shoulders in the Greta Garbo style; complexions had the paleness of a Marlene Dietrich and lips, the redness of Joan Crawford's.

Fur jackets were cut in an infinite variety of ways. Some had asymmetrical flaps, others shaped-panels or groups of pleats in front or behind in order to increase their fullness.

Evening coats, which had been worn short for years and in which Eve's daughters had shivered with a smile, suddenly lengthened and even acquired a comfortable woollen lining...

By daytime, women were still able to breathe freely... Little did they realize their good fortune! Rochas was about to launch his famous wasp-waist which thrilled women throughout the world even though it also prevented most of them from breathing. But who cared? Suffering was no new experience to coquettes!

Pierre Balmain had not yet discovered his "Jolie Madame", but was already on the path to success

Opulant years were typical at the period. The coats were created in the mid-Twenties. (Bibliothèque Nationale.)

and meanwhile much fuss was being made of another young and daring dress-designer, Jacques Fath, who launched the barrel-skirt and printed dresses recalling those Indian shawls so dear to our grandmothers. Princess-dresses reappeared in muslin, organza or brocaded taffeta...

Hats became more and more daring. Agnes launched the letter-hat, closed like an envelope and sealed with red wax. Suzy launched the straw boater while Rose Valois preferred it covered with cloth. Louis XV tricorns, "Bonaparte" up-turned hats, "coach-driver's" top-hats... all these and many more made their appearance.

Shoes became square-toed and were worn over smoky grey stockings which showed off the leg to best advantage.

Crinolines — so dear to our grandmothers — were once more worn beneath skirts and the grand spring balls reminded one of the ostentation which had prevailed during the Second Empire. Waltzes became fashionable again and suddenly fans made a brief appearance at the window. Roger Faré also created gloves, embroidered in the old-fashioned style (for Hermès), and parasols with silken fringes made a reappearance.

Lord Chamberlain was responsible for making round-handled umbrellas fashionable and these have remained to the present-day a symbol of English and French male elegance. Jacques Heim launched the pareo and beach pyjamas. "Slacks" — sport trousers

— were much in vogue at Deauville, Cannes and on millionaires' yachts.

In 1939, as always when war is approaching, when human beings sense catastrophe like dogs scent an earthquake, and no longer know either what they want or where they are heading, fashion adopted the "amusing" or "idealistic" styles! In the evenings, extra tight sheaths were worn (signed Balenciaga), outsized crinolines (signed Lanvin), Greek drapés (signed Grès) along with outrageous or prudish décolletés. Hats were huge: velvet halos, large flat boaters, enveloping capes (signed Reboux). All these were both slightly mad and very pretty.

The war found sun-tanned holiday-makers wearing loud-colored pagnes, leafy two-pieces which looked more like music-hall costumes than bathing suits.

World War II broke out in 1939 — and France adapted itself. Robert Piguet king of the "little", very elegant, dress, created a "shelter-outfit" of thick woollen material, with wide trousers and a long cape with a hood. Hermès offered a suit with deep pockets suitable for cycling, while Paulette launched a turban to cover the ears. Nina Ricci offered protection to the elegant woman in the shape of a coat with a wide collar and a little drum hat tied beneath the chin with a scarf, and a muff for the hands. Balenciaga wrapped foxes around those sensitive to the cold and designed hostess gowns which were as warm as they were elegant. The summer brought with it the peasant dress, the gardener's apron and

What thinness, what length, what fragility!

Fashion, incarnating itself in these sense less creatures,

becomes rather abstract.

blue boiler-suits. Rochas changed the silhouette by introducing rounded shoulders, a slim waist and wide, knee-length skirts.

The Occupation, with its restrictions, gave birth to a new state of mind which encouraged the Parisian woman to flout the occupying power. She appeared decked out in dresses thirty feet wide, cut out of ersatz materials, and hats as fancy as you could wish. Albouy's newspaper boaters, Madame Agnes's turbans made out of wood-shavings, Reboux's fibre-cloth hats, the bonnet-cum-haircurlers of Gilbert Orcel (consisting of a scarf and paper) intended for coquettes stranded at the hairdresser during an electricity break-down. Electric torches were concealed in umbrella-handles or in the thick wooden soles of shoes, while sub-machine guns were hidden in shopping baskets beneath cabbages or turnips.

Bridge was the order of the evening, and people went to bridge-parties on bicycles with their sequin-decorated pockets turned inside-out so as not to attract attention in the street.

Little by little, hats slipped from fantasy to absurdity. Female cyclists of 1943 were weighed down beneath beribboned mops, flowered blunderbusses, crumpled straw pumpkins, apple-charlottes of curly netting, all ridiculous beyond words. Added to this, co-quettes felt it necessary to wear earrings as enormous as they were loud such as regular Sicilian mules' tassels which brushed not only their cheeks but also their shoulders.

Two dresses by Jean Dessès.

The suits on these two pages were designed by (left to right) Mandel, Raphël, Madeleine de Rauch and Charles Montaigne. (L'Officiel de la Couture.)

White hands love the work of others

Stockings disappeared but were replaced by a kind of sock with clogs four inches high, the soles more or less hinged.

The genius of Parisian shoe-makers was such that, in spite of the lack of leather, thread and nails, their shoes were charming. They made use of the most unexpected materials : cork, raffia, felt, rabbit fur, straw, fireman's hose, sailor's rope and perhaps even cow-horns and hen's beaks ? But the results were such that, after the Liberation, the Americans were so taken with these little works of art that they enthusiastically copied them !

The rabbit was king. He literally saved the day ! He was put to every conceivable use. Not only was he eaten, but he was shaved, lustred, dyed and was served up as otter, chinchilla, nutria and even mink... People also threw themselves upon wild-fowl, foxes, martens, weasels, squirrels and moles to protect themselves from the cold.

Then came the Liberation at last. Everyone kissed the Americans and the fashion became red, white and blue like their flag. For a few months, everything was colored in blue, white or red. During the winter, "Royal Air Force" blue and khaki became fashionable. For a year, there were only artificial colors : sea-greens, old pinks, purplish-reds and kerosene-blues. Suits remained classic, jackets long and dresses short.

Jacques Fath's imagination burst out like a firework display. He dazzled all with his luxurious materials out of which he cut dresses which matched the linings of his coats. For evening-wear, he recalled romantic gracefulness, long-sleeved bodices and rustling skirts in the Madame Bovary style.

Mademoiselle Carven was much talked of. Being very small herself, she only designed for smaller women. She had taste, wit and talent.

Jacques Griffe made a name for himself. His models were elegant and easy to wear. His evening-dresses were enchanting creations in tulle.

THE FOURTEENTH REVOLUTION

CHRISTIAN DIOR

It was in 1947 that Dior's star first made its appearance in the sky of Haute Couture. It immediately became the brightest in the sky — almost before it had appeared, one might say. Never had a seemingly unknown dress-designer been so discussed. Everybody wanted to attend his first showing. It was a scramble and a rush. The seats were numbered as in a theatre, the salesgirls were turned into usherettes, the press was packed as far back as the staircase, photographers were crowded into the corners like flies in the fall, bouquets of flowers cast dazzling reflections into the mirrors of the rooms and a gentle perfume filled the air. It was the first time that such a Haute Couture showing was presented with such a display of luxury. Even the names of the slim mannequins whom the new star had chosen to launch his new fashion were known beforehand : Tania, Yolande, Noëlle, Marie-Thérèse and Paule. Everyone knew that the master's mascot was Bobby, his dog (each season, one of the dresses was named

MINI-SKIRTS AND MAXI-BOOTS

after him), and lily-of-the-valley, his lucky charm. Whenever he held a showing, admirers from all over the world would send him some. Less well-known was the fact that a small piece of metal, in the shape of a horse-shoe, always hung in his office; he had picked it up in the street the day he said "yes" to Marcel Boussac.

Within forty-eight hours, France and America were swearing only by Dior. His "new-look" revolutionized Parisian women who, from one day to the next, refused to wear anything but swirling dresses with ankle-length hem-lines, closely-fitted jackets with wavy panels over the hips, and rounded shoulders. And the man who succeeded in revolutionizing fashion throughout the world? Dior was a quiet and peaceful individual with gentle eyes, a weak chin and sensitive mouth. His movements were measured, he never seemed to be in a hurry. The atmosphere in his office was calm and neat. No patterns or drawings hung on the wall. He refused to allow his conversations to be interrupted by incessant telephone calls, nor by secretaries eager to obtain his signature or an order.

Dior was first and foremost an artist; he liked music, painting and sculpture. He dreamed of becoming an architect. Finally, between 1928 and 1932, he

directed, with a friend, Pierre Coll, the "Dior and Coll" art gallery in the rue Cambacérès and there made the acquaintance of Christian Bérard, Cocteau, Dali and of so many other artistic personalities who were to influence or help him later on.

At that time, he had not as yet done any drawing. "I am much too fond of art and respect it too much for that!" he would say jokingly. But finally, in 1932, business was not very bright and he joined Piguet as a designer. From 1940 to 1946, he worked with Lucien Lelong. This was where he first met the famous Raymonde who was "studio assistant" to the dressmaker. She was to follow Dior to the avenue Montaigne and remained thereafter the power behind the throne, organizing mannequin parades, directing the workshops and finding for him, the right button, the rare material, the unobtainable lace... It was she who arranged everything, smoothing out all difficulties.

BIRTH OF THE HOUSE OF DIOR

In 1947, Marcel Boussac, the textile magnate, was looking around for a fashion house which he could finance in order to launch a fabric promotion campaign. Christian Dior's name was raised. The two men got on together immediately. Boussac put him

(From left to right):

Three dresses by Pierre Cardin.

A dress by Christian Dior. (L'Officiel de la Couture.)

" Beat your wife every morning,
if you don't know why, she does. "
Arab proverb

(From left to right):
Cardin ensemble.

Pierre Balmain ensemble.

A dress by Cardin.
(L'Officiel de la Couture.)

in charge of the new business although he could not possibly have foreseen that the deal he was concluding would be so successful thanks to his partner's masterly handling of it. An attentive and clairvoyant businessman was hidden beneath the artist.

Dior built up a dress as one would a palace, by mixing materials and using them in different directions. To him, "straight thread" represented classicism and "slanting thread" baroque. He considered these two "directions" indispensable to creation in the same way that gravity is the basis of it.

Without actually going as far as using a plumb-line when cutting out his models, Christian Dior conformed to this law. He also insisted that ornamentation, although having lost its symbolic value, remained an integral part of the dress just as mouldings, frontons and relief, or bas-relief, friezes are inseparable from the monuments upon which they have been placed.

When asked how a fashion asserts itself nowadays, he replied that dress-designers make use of ideas which are in the air just as do contemporary novelists and playwrights.

"One fashion comes as a reaction to the preceding one and changing it is a delicate business, practically a matter of conscience," Dior explained in his memoirs. "The most successful ones are those which develop the slowest and I always try to distinguish between what one no longer likes, what one still likes and what one is about to like." This is how he explained the "common ground" on which all designers meet in the same spirit, despite the fact that each is working on his own in secret. "One never does anything voluntarily," he wrote, "and fashions are no exception to the rule. Ideas are born like flowers."

And it was perhaps because young American women found postwar fashions "outdated" for them and wore little blouses with wide skirts strangled at the waist, that the "New Look" idea "floated" in the air.

Dior maintained that the short knee-length skirt was most unaesthetic and anti-feminine. However, since a dress must also be practical, it could be wider when it is long for "a fettered woman can never have an attractive walk." According to him, women should be graceful, supple, slinky and a little precious. Christian Dior had such a sense of style, of refinement and balance that some of his models literally make one cry out in admiration. One gazes at them as if at a drawing by Ingres or a painting by Velasquez. His ensembles, whether plain or luxurious, always have that spark of genius which gives, even to a shirt-dress, the "Dior style".

He launched the idea of "outfits", including gloves, shoes, hats, stockings, bags — all carrying his personal mark. The idea of making "fancy jewellery" to serve as a complement to dresses was also his. He thought of everything, created girdles which

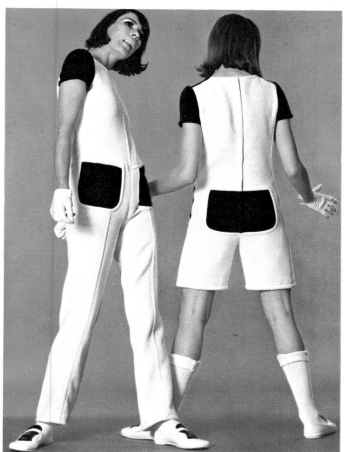

modified the silhouette either by hollowing the stomach or filling in the side so as to lengthen the bust line. His bras lifted the bosom in order to round it out. He even thought up a new ensemble for evening wear: bra-and-suspenders made of gold thread in a washable and stainless material.

Styles Were Given Names Just Like the Models

The mid-century brought with it a little spell of madness. Gowns were graphically described: the "scissors" line at Dior's, the "gushing" line at Fath's, the "Torpedo" at Paquin's, "stop and go" at Schiaparelli's, "Roly-poly" at Jeanne Lafaurie's, "Cockle-Shell" at Lanvin's, "Looping" at Rochas, "Eiffel Tower" at Bruyère's, "Lassoo" at Jean Desses', "breath of Spring" at Madeleine Vramant's, "Holy Year" at Carven's, "Mushroom" at Piguet's, "Helicopter" at Jacques Heim's.

The main characteristics of that period consisted of straight dresses, from which hung panels, puffs, pleated scallops, wrap-overs or fold-backs and materials treated in many other ways so as to create an illusion. Shoulders were drooping, belts were curved down at the back, sleeves were very short or puffed and skirts were 15 inches off the ground. For the evening, ball-dresses of the "ballerina" type, coming above the ankle, competed with the "mermaid" style or crinolines.

Balenciaga made a special name for himself in Haute Couture. Dior had his admirers, and so did the Spanish designer who was a genius too. His "little suits", his coats, his grand evening gowns were matchless. His carefully prepared fittings attained to perfection.

One of his pupils, Hubert de Givenchy, began to be talked of. His technique was remarkable; he was young and his models were full of the freshness of youth. Jean Dessès, of Greek origin, revealed himself to be an excellent dress-designer, while Castillo, at Lanvin's, was highly successful and rapidly became a byword for elegance. Balmain created his "Jolie Madame" style which he was to follow from one year to the next. Although he rarely made fashion history, the beautiful women who became his clients always remained faithful to him.

Young Guy Laroche also made a name for himself after setting up business in the Avenue Montaigne. His ideas were good and so was his cut. He revived the fashion for dresses covered with pearls, so convenient for women who travelled and wished to be smart since they required no ironing.

(From left to right):
Courrèges ensemble

Coat by Pierre Cardin

Ensemble by Courrèges.
(L'Officiel de la Couture.)

" The young are made to believe that stars exist with projecting breasts and free moonlight, all the oxygen you want, and passportless space, but it is not true."

Raymond Queneau

Others, younger still, made their mark with the younger set and the starlets. Louis Féraud, Jacques Esterel and particularly Ted Lapidus with his male and female ready-to-wear, were to make names for themselves. Paco Raban should also be mentioned, for he created a new mode with his metallic discs linked together to make dresses.

Special mention should be made of the Italian dress-designer Pucci who has been in France now for several years and has transformed the winter and summer sports fashions with very attractive personal colors and designs.

Finally, we should note a sensational come-back, that of Coco Chanel who, at an age where most people generally give up, launched a new fashion, astonishingly youthful and hailed with enthusiasm by smart women throughout the world. Her wonderful lamé suits for evening-wear and her wool-piped costumes for morning wear caused a small revolution on their own.

THE FIFTEENTH REVOLUTION

The Mini-Skirt or Where Do We Go From Here... How did this saucy garment come to be such a success? In 1961, when Pierre Cardin first showed dresses which revealed knees and boots which hid them, fashionable women said to themselves, "Couturiers may suggest but we women decide. We shall never wear these very short skirts and boots designed for riding to the hounds, we will never swallow that sort of bait."

Yet, less than four years later, they were doing just that, swallowing it hook, line and sinker. It was Pierre Cardin who first launched the idea, albeit in supple lines, that is, soft materials such as lightweight woollens, satins and crêpes. The mind and eye adapted to this version and the path was paved for another revolution.

Courrèges, with his extraordinary vitality and enthusiasm, took over and launched the revolution, carrying it right into the street. His geometrical style was youthful, cut out of stiff woollen materials and done in light colors.

By wearing his designs or their copies, American women launched the fashion for skirts above the knee. Miss Mary Quant, the charming British designer, nelped to tum the staid London streets into a wild carnival. In Paris, the sweet young things strolled along the Boulevard Saint-Germain in skirts skimming their posteriors while their male counterparts sported romantic costumes in strange colors.

Three star designers have contributed to this 15th revolution : Pierre Cardin and André Courrèges, already mentioned, and Yves Saint-Laurent. In this age when extremes in elegance and avant-garde fashions are within the reach of any purse, it is interesting to see how these three reached the pinnacle of Paris Haute Couture

PIERRE CARDIN

Tall, slim, seemingly frail, his face is young yet furrowèd. He has a serious sensuous mouth and a straight nose quivering between a pair of grey-green, often anxious, eyes. He wears short sideburns and his hair is slightly dishevelled. His voice is soft and strangely surprising.

While still young, he was attracted to architecture but the war interrupted his studies. He then settled in Paris where he met Cocteau and Christian Bérard who invited him to work with Marcel Escoffier on the costumes for "Beauty and the Beast" and the "Two-Headed Eagle" which paved the way for his career. He joined Paquin and then Schiaparelli for a time, then when Christian Dior opened his house, he chose Cardin to help him prepare the "New Look". Six years later, he set out on his own, opening his business in two attic rooms on the rue Richepanse, where he made only suits and coats. By 1956, Cardin was on the Faubourg Saint-Honoré, where he opened a shop for men's clothing accessories which he quickly divided in two to accommodate a few trifles for women as well.

In 1957, he started to create loose-fitting gowns for afternoon wear, cocktails and for the evening. The "balloon" dress with a tarlatan lining which he launched at that time brought customers and the press to his showrooms in a rush. He became a recognized creator of fashions.

In 1959, he started his "ready-mades" and in 1962, he decided to try his hand at a "Modern Man" style by setting up a male workshop.

The following year, a suit manufacturer from Orleans, France, suggested that Cardin design a junior collection. This turned out to be a triumph. Not only did the teenagers seek a new silhouette but their elders did as well. It was a masculine revolution copied every where,

At the present time his business is world-wide and his success continually increases for his Haute Couture creations as well as for his boutiques for men and women.

ANDRE COURREGES

This designer is 43 years old. A direct, forthright gentlemen, he assures us that he would change his religion to achieve his goal if such was necessary. But apparently, he has not had to go that far for success arrived first. His name is as famous as his colors are acid and his designs geometrical. He can now even been seen in the Grévin Museum in Paris where famous people are modelled in wax. *Chez* Courrèges, everything is white. His square pouffs, his walls, carpets, lamps and sales-girls' dresses. He himself, lord of the mini-skirt, is often dressed like a tennis player with a roll-neck sweater, shoes, socks and trousers, all white, white, white. Only his dark eyes twinkle. He loves gaiety and his mannequins show off his models while dancing to popular tunes. Courrèges took to fashion like a duck to water. At the age of 25, after studying to be a civil engineer,

(From left to right):

Coat by Cardin.

Dior ensemble.

Yves Saint-Laurent ensemble.
(L'Officiel de la Couture.)

Cardin dress. (Photo P. Cardin.)

" *It's a girl of today, that is,*

almost a young man of yesterday."

Paul Morand

he went up to Paris and joined Jeanne Lafaurie. Six months later he was much attracted by Balenciaga's style but the Spanish master did not need a designer at the time. Nevertheless he was interested by this young man who cut his own clothes and made socks out of a jersey material because he could not find socks to his liking. Balenciaga therefore took him on as an apprentice and Courrèges remained with him for ten years.

On Sundays, the young couturier played football with a Paris club team, but if he tried to shoot goals, it was mainly with regard to fashion. He wanted to give women freedom of body and comfortable simplicity. He pondered on the problems of working women and refused to accept either girdles or high heels. Neither did he encourage the mid-calf dress but preferred skirts which freed leg and knee, and shod feet in comfortable little boots.

He set up business on the Avenue Kléber. His first collections were successful because they were young and gay but he was not yet ready for the hard punch which he wanted to give fashion. It was not until 1965 that he triggered off his shock campaign and revolutionized fashion.

Courrèges has been copied and plagiarized more than any other dress-designer and this is the reason for his wishing to establish a large-scale modern sales system.

"The development of an automobile prototype costs between 300 and 400 million francs," he explains. "Mine are costly too and they are reproduced to the nearest millimetre. Dress-making should remain a hand-craft. Each of my designs is reproduced in five sizes and all the physiological characteristics are taken into account. The quality is high. I would like to see the day when the women who buy their clothes from me no longer worry about their figures, and feel as young at sixty as they do at thirty."

Courrèges is not only a dress-designer, he is also a magician and a visionary. He builds his dresses rather than designing them, and is carried away by a fabric in a wave of enthusiasm. His models are geometric, and can be outlined by a square, a trapezoid or a triangle. Always busily inventing, he does not hesitate to transform a woman into an orange zebra or a black and white chess-board. The kind of woman who dreams of strolling on Venus or racing to Mars should be dressed by Courrèges, although the designer does not ascribe to this label, "designer for outer space".

"Women," he says, "should have children, go shopping, get in and out of cars, buses, subways, planes, go dancing, work, be young, dynamic, emancipated, always active and beautiful or there is something wrong with them."

YVES SAINT-LAURENT

Christian Dior called him "the Little Prince". In actual fact, he is very tall, very thin, and apparently very shy. But beneath this reserve, Yves Saint-Laurent has a strong character, a great capacity for

work and an extraordinary will to conquer. He was born in Oran, Algeria, of a family of lawyers but from earliest childhood, he was passionately interested by theater and fashion, far more so than by law. At sixteen, after having passed his exams, he left Oran for Paris. Being gifted in drawing, he was already sketching dresses, and decided to attend a dress-making school. But he left in a huff when he was told to make a straw mannequin. In 1953, he entered a dress-designing competition and won first prize with his cocktail dress design. He was then 17 years old.

Michel de Brunhoff, Paris director of *Vogue*, then introduced him to Christian Dior on the eve of the latter's new collection. Dior was impressed by Saint-Laurent's drawings, all the more so because they embodied the general characteristics of his new forthcoming trend. Saint-Laurent had sensed the new fashion as a thoroughbred dog senses game from afar. Christian Dior took him on and for four years, Saint-Laurent was his right-hand man. After Dior's death, Boussac asked him to take over. Saint-Laurent was 21 years old. From one day to the next, he became head of a business of more than 2000 people. But far from losing his head, he worked harder than ever. He was solicited from every side but this youngest ever dress-designer took refuge in apparent shyness. His reticence paid off for his first "line", the "trapeze" was a success and put him in the limelight.

In 1960, the army claimed him, but once out in 1962, he set himself up in business. His first collection was a success, and he dressed elegant women from all over the world. He was then free to design for the Roland Petit ballet, *Cyrano de Bergerac*. His haute couture collections are always spectacular, often revolutionary and not always easy to wear for the not so young. The "Little Prince" is very much

(From left to right):

A dress and coat by Pierre Cardin.

The "Pierre Cardin" fashion.
(L'Officiel de la Couture.)

The "cosmonaut" fashion.
(Photos Pierre Cardin.)

in vogue and admits that the Courrèges revolution
has greatly stimulated him. He too has his boutique
on the Left Bank where the stars of stage and screen
come to dress and all at the age of thirty.

AND TOMORROW?

Can the styles of this latest revolution be called a
fashion? Are they elegant? Yes to the first question because everyone wears them. As to the second
question, it must be admitted that these clothes have
little in common with the styles launched in the past
by an artistic prince, a king's mistress, a travel-loving
sultan or a capricious courtesan. Is this sufficient
reason for rejoicing? Yes, mainly because there are
no longer those awesome barriers between the court
with its privileged members and the rest of the
world. Little by little, the differences have been
levelled out. However, the gap between those with
money and those without will always exist, and the

moneyed class will always dominate. Unfortunately, gold is not always synonymous with good taste. The art of dressing, of choosing with taste a "line" or "silhouette" for oneself is not a gift possessed by everyone nor is it easy to acquite.

Today, two fashion trends exist : that of the Haute Couture or custom-made, and that of the Boutique or ready-made. The two are not always compatible in my estimation, for while it is quite normal that everybody can be dressed by couturiers who create custom collections and boutique models in the same styles, it seems to me inadmissible that customers who pay hundreds of dollars in order to have the pleasure of wearing a work of art should see an almost identical model come out in ready-to-wear at a price accessible to all.

Dress-designing has obviously undergone great changes but could we not return to the idea of an exclusive design even if it only concerns the material ? A dress should never be repeated twice in the same

material except for foreign customers. Why not produce numbered copies as in the case of limited editions of books — five cocktail dresses in crêpe, seven in satin, three in lamé — it would be a snobbery worth cultivating. Mrs. X when deciding on number 4 would be told that Mrs. A, B, and C have the same one which might encourage her to choose a different model or to ask the designer to give her 4 an original touch.

The 15th revolution is upon us. We are living it. What will the 16th be like ? A long skirt, no doubt, worn by an ultra-feminine woman. Men will be more "dressed-up", that is to say, more elegant and less classic, without, however, appearing terribly overdressed.

Should my readers wish to know — after reading about these millennia of revolutions — what I consider to be the ideal fashion, I would say that it is that of 1830 : slim waist, low-neckline, wide skirt and buskins.

Contents

Index to illustrations

Bibliographical index

ETRUSCAN ART
   Raymond Bloc. Bibliothèque des Arts.

ART AND THE ETRUSCAN CIVILIZATION
   Plon.

THE HISTORY OF COSTUME
   F. Boucher. Flammarion.

HOW TO RECOGNIZE STYLES, FROM THE VIIITH TO THE XIXTH CENTURIES
   M. Comment. Hachette.

FIVE THOUSAND YEARS OF ELEGANCE
   Mme Desroche-Noblecourt. Hachette.

THE LIFE AND DEATH OF A PHAROAH
   Mme Desroche-Noblecourt. Hachette.

THE FRANKS IN ARCHAEOLOGY
   J.P. Eydoux. Plon.

ORIENTAL COSTUME IN ANTIQUITY
   J. Heuzey. Champion.

COSTUMES FROM TUDOR TIMES TO LOUIS XVI
   James Laver. Horizon de France.

FEMALE UNDER-GARMENTS
   Cécil .Saint-Laurent. Plon.

ANCIENT MEXICAN ART
   J. Soustelle. Arthaud.

A HISTORY OF FASHION
   M. Wilhem. Hachette

A Studio Hachette publication

ART DIRECTOR
Philippe Cheverny

LAYOUT
Danielle Troubat

PICTURE RESEARCH
Maggy Cheverny

PHOTO ENGRAVING
directed by
Émile Golaz

Printed on
matt art paper Matador 7
from the Navarre Mills
by Georges Lang, Paris
September, 1968.

Dépôt légal 3e trimestre 1968. No 128.